Learning IoT with Particle Photon and Electron

Develop applications on one of the most popular platforms for IoT using Particle Photon and Electron with this fast-paced guide

Rashid Khan
Kajari Ghoshdastidar
Ajith Vasudevan

BIRMINGHAM - MUMBAI

Learning IoT with Particle Photon and Electron

First published: September 2016

Production reference: 1070916

Published by Packt Publishing Ltd.
Livery Place
35 Livery Street
Birmingham
B3 2PB, UK.
ISBN 978-1-78588-529-7

www.packtpub.com

Credits

Authors

Rashid Khan
Kajari Ghoshdastidar
Ajith Vasudevan

Commissioning Editor

Neil Alexander

Acquisition Editors

Aaron Lazar
Reshma Raman

Content Development Editor

Pooja Mhapsekar

Technical Editor

Sunith Shetty

Copy Editor

Sonia Mathur

Project Coordinator

Suzanne Coutinho

Proofreader

Safis Editing

Indexer

Rekha Nair

Graphics

Jason Monteiro

Production Coordinator

Aparna Bhagat

About the Authors

Rashid Khan is a programmer living in Bangalore. He is one of the founders of Yellow Messenger, a company that specializes in building bots for commerce. Prior to founding Yellow Messenger, he worked at EdgeVerve Systems, where he built backend systems to support IoT devices. He is an open source enthusiast and loves to experiment with new technologies. He is involved with a number of open source organizations, such as GNOME, Mono, Tomboy Notes, and Banshee and has built a Django (Python) library for Apache Spark called Django-LibSpark.

His interests lie in the field of Artificial Intelligence and interfacing software with real-world objects. Apart from programming, he loves to cycle and play tennis.

I am really thankful to my mother and father for providing the motivation and guidance to help me push myself constantly. My co-founders at Yellow Messenger, Anik, Raghu, and Kishore, provided constant support to experiment with new ideas for this book, and I would like to extend my gratitude for that. I would like to thank Rajeshwari Ganesan, my manager at EdgeVerve Systems, for giving me the opportunity to author this book. I would like to extend my gratitude to Ajith and Kajari, my coauthors, without whom this book would not be possible. This book would be incomplete without the guidance and mentorship of my friends and co-workers at EdgeVerve. I am extremely thankful to Chetan, who helped a lot with the sensors and data, and Nelly (Jeonghyun Kang), who helped with the firmware and testing out the initial projects.

Kajari Ghoshdastidar got her PhD in wireless sensor networks in 2009 and has been active in IoT-related hobby project work since then. She has worked in the software industry for the last 6 years as a technology architect, software developer, and a computer scientist. She is a technology geek, takes part in hackathons, and is always exploring new technologies and electronic gadgets.

She is currently part of the systems engineering team at EdgeVerve, working as a computer scientist.

First of all, I would like to thank Rajeshwari Ganesan, my mentor and manager at Edgeverve, for inspiring me to pen this book and closely guiding me all the way, and Rashid and Ajith for being the most awesome coauthors I could wish for. This book wouldn't be complete without the support of my colleagues at Edgeverve, Chetan Kumar Velumurugan, who helped us a lot with his deep knowledge of sensors and accessories, and Nelly (Jeonghyun Kang), who helped with setting up and testing out the initial projects.

Ajith Vasudevan is an electronics, computer, and IoT enthusiast who likes to apply his knowledge in these fields to make modern living easy for himself and others around him. He has a bachelor's of technology degree in electrical and electronics engineering. He was interested in automation and IoT even before the term IoT became commonplace. He designed and built an automatic overhead-tank motor operator using $1 worth of electronic parts back in 1995, which is operating at his parent's home to this day. He has automated and made it simple and efficient to operate many household appliances, for example, an automatic geyser switch that turns itself off after 10 minutes, saving electricity. It can be set to switch on at any specified time or can be controlled from anywhere. Today, even his friends and neighbors use this system.

Ajith has worked in the heavy electrical industry before joining his current employer, Infosys Technologies Limited, in the year 2000. He is presently a senior computer scientist at EdgeVerve Systems, a subsidiary of Infosys. At work, he enjoys programming and has done so for over a decade and a half.

I would like to thank Rajeshwari Ganesan for introducing me to the coauthors and Packt Publishing and for giving me the opportunity to coauthor this book. It has been an enjoyable and great learning experience for me.

www.PacktPub.com

eBooks, discount offers, and more

Did you know that Packt offers eBook versions of every book published, with PDF and ePub files available? You can upgrade to the eBook version at www.PacktPub.com and as a print book customer, you are entitled to a discount on the eBook copy. Get in touch with us at customercare@packtpub.com for more details.

At www.PacktPub.com, you can also read a collection of free technical articles, sign up for a range of free newsletters and receive exclusive discounts and offers on Packt books and eBooks.

https://www2.packtpub.com/books/subscription/packtlib

Do you need instant solutions to your IT questions? PacktLib is Packt's online digital book library. Here, you can search, access, and read Packt's entire library of books.

Why subscribe?

- Fully searchable across every book published by Packt
- Copy and paste, print, and bookmark content
- On demand and accessible via a web browser

Table of Contents

Preface   1

Chapter 1: Introducing IoT with Particle Photon and Electron   7

  Evolution of the IoT   8
    Why the IoT has become a household word now   8
  Hardware and software in the IoT ecosystem   8
    Essential terminology   9
    Network protocols   10
  Market survey of IoT development boards and cloud services   11
    IoT development boards   12
    Cloud services (PaaS, BaaS, M2M)   13
  What is Particle?   14
    The journey of Particle   14
    Why Particle?   15
    What does Particle offer?   16
  Photon, Electron, and Core   16
    Spark Core   17
    Particle Photon   17
    Particle Electron   19
    Comparison   20
  Summary   21

Chapter 2: Fire Up Your Kit   23

  Essentials of FreeRTOS and hardware resources   24
  Flow diagram for the Twitter project   27
  Getting the Photon online   28
    Setting up the Photon or Core   28
    Software and hardware requirements   29
    Software setup   29
    Connecting Particle Photon or Core   31
    The Web IDE   32
  Twitter and e-mail interaction project   34
    Setting up a Twitter developer account   34
    Sending web requests using Particle webhooks   35
    Creating a webhook   35
    Listing and deleting webhooks   36

Putting it all together   37
Setting up the Twitter and e-mail webhook   37
How to sense motion?   40
Sensing button presses – programming the buttons   42
Tweets and e-mail   43
Troubleshooting   48
Summary   49

Chapter 3: P2P and Local Server   51
Client-server versus P2P networks ÂÂ   51
Traditional client-server architecture   51
Peer-to-peer network architecture   52
Client-server versus P2P   53
Advantages and disadvantages of P2P networking   53
Setting up a P2P network for Particle devices   54
Flash the VoodooSpark firmware   54
Connect the Particle board with VoodooSpark   54
Controlling your Particle board using the keyboard   55
Local server setup   57
Advantages and disadvantages of Particle local server   58
Installing Particle server on a local machine   58
Configuring the local server   59
Alternate protocols for IoT   62
MQTT   62
CoAP   62
Summary   64

Chapter 4: Connecting the Sensors   65
Overview of the project   65
Hardware components and setup   66
RFID reader module RC522-RFID and RFID tags   67
PIR motion sensor   68
Data flow diagrams   70
Communication between the Photons   72
Sample code   73
Photon with the RFID reader   75
Photon with the motion sensor   78
Data storage on the cloud   79
Cloud data analysis and SMS notification   83
Troubleshooting   84
Summary   86

Chapter 5: Of Cars and Controllers   87

Building the model car – hardware components   88
Wheels   88
L293D motor driver   89
65 RPM DC Right Angled motor   90
Chassis   91
Power supply and Li-Po battery   91
Breadboard and jumper wires   91
Building the model car – prerequisites   93
Putting it all together and controlling the car   93
The code   95
Running the program and controlling the car   99
Moving the car with gestures   100
How it works   100
The code   101
Programming the car with the Electron   102
Putting it all together (again)   102
The code   104
Troubleshooting   105
Summary   106

Chapter 6: Hacking the Firmware   107

What is firmware?   107
A bit of history   108
Obtaining and flashing firmware   108
Obtaining firmware   109
Obtaining firmware by direct download   109
Obtaining firmware by building from source   110
ARM GCC   110
Make   111
Git   112
Getting the firmware source code   112
Compiling the code   112
Burning firmware onto the device   113
Burning firmware using the OTA method   113
Burning firmware using Particle-CLI   114
Burning firmware using the DFU-Util method   115
Installing DFU-Util   115
Flashing firmware   117
Custom firmware   118
Summary   119

Preface

Devices made by Particle (the IoT company formerly known as Spark) are one of the most popular IoT platforms for hobbyists and professionals alike. This fast-paced guide will help you develop IoT-based applications using two of Particle's popular boards—the Photon and the Electron.

What this book covers

Chapter 1, *Introducing IoT with Particle Photon and Electron*, introduces you to IoT and common hardware and software used in building IoT projects, and lists popular IoT boards. The chapter then introduces Particle, the IoT company, and describes its three main products—the Photon, the Electron, and the Core.

Chapter 2, *Fire Up Your Kit*, gives a brief introduction to the workings of FreeRTOS, the operating system of Photon. The chapter goes on to help you build a Twitter and email-interaction project. You will learn to code for Photon using ParticleJS in the web-based IDE called Particle Build.

Chapter 3, *P2P and Local Server*, compares two popular network architectures used in IoT projects and shows you how to set up a P2P network for Particle devices. This chapter also describes how to set up a local server to make communication between devices faster. Finally, we will introduce you to other popular protocols and architectures used in IoT.

Chapter 4, *Connecting the Sensors*, shows you how to build a smart kitchen using a network of Photons with cloud-based data storage, analysis, and notifications using webhooks.

Chapter 5, *Of Cars and Controllers*, teaches you how to use Photon and Electron to build a connected model car that is capable of being controlled remotely using a keyboard. We will also show you how to modify this project to control the car by hand gestures using a Leap Motion controller.

Chapter 6, *Hacking the Firmware*, talks about the role of firmware in the Particle devices and shows you different ways to obtain and deploy the firmware on them. We will also list the advantages of custom firmware, taking the case of the VoodooSpark custom firmware as an example.

What you need for this book

This book describes various IoT projects that you will want to try out. In order to successfully execute these projects, the following software needs to be installed on your computer:

- Linux (preferable) or the Windows operating system.
- eBook reader helps you open the eBook version of this book on your computer for ease of copying code snippets to and from the book to your code editor on the computer.
- A text editor, such as GEdit (Linux) or Notepad++ (Windows), to edit the code locally.
- A web browser to access and use a web-based code editor and to download software.
- Node.js (https://www.nodejs.org)—a JavaScript runtime built on Chrome's V8 JavaScript engine.
- Particle CLI (https://docs.particle.io/guide/tools-and-features/cli/photon/)—a command-line interface from Particle.
- Particle driver for Windows is required only if you're using Windows OS. For more information, see https://docs.particle.io/guide/getting-started/connect/photon/, and look for the *Installing the Particle driver* section.
- Cylon.js (https://cylonjs.com/)—a JavaScript framework for robotics, physical computing, and IoT.
- ARM GCC—an ARM variant of the GCC compiler tool chain for the C language.
- make, a command-line utility that compiles and builds binaries from source code.
- Git, a distributed version-control system.

  The *Obtaining firmware by building from source* section of Chapter 6, *Hacking the Firmware*, describes how you can obtain ARM GCC, make, and Git for Windows, Linux, and Mac OS.

- DFU-Util (http://dfu-Util.sourceforge.net/)—a utility to download and upload firmware to/from devices connected over USB.

  The *Burning firmware using the DFU-Util method* section of Chapter 6, *Hacking the Firmware*, describes how you can obtain DFU-Util for Windows, Linux, and Mac OS.

Who this book is for

This book is for developers, IoT enthusiasts, and hobbyists who want to enhance their knowledge of IoT machine-to-machine architecture using Particle Photon and Electron and implement cloud-based IoT projects.

Conventions

In this book, you will find a number of text styles that distinguish between different kinds of information. Here are some examples of these styles and an explanation of their meaning.

Code words in text, database table names, folder names, filenames, file extensions, pathnames, dummy URLs, user input, and Twitter handles are shown as follows: "The driver is called `spark_core.cat`."

A block of code is set as follows:

```
{
    "event": "twitterFetch",
    "url": "https://api.twitter.com/1.1/search/tweets.json",
    "requestType": "GET",
    "headers": {
        "Authorization" : "Bearer XXXXXX"
    },
```

Any command-line input or output is written as follows:

```
$ particle setup
```

New terms and **important words** are shown in bold. Words that you see on the screen, for example, in menus or dialog boxes, appear in the text like this: "Select the **Advanced** tab."

Warnings or important notes appear in a box like this.

Tips and tricks appear like this.

Reader feedback

Feedback from our readers is always welcome. Let us know what you think about this book-what you liked or disliked. Reader feedback is important for us as it helps us develop titles that you will really get the most out of. To send us general feedback, simply e-mail `feedback@packtpub.com`, and mention the book's title in the subject of your message. If there is a topic that you have expertise in and you are interested in either writing or contributing to a book, see our author guide at `www.packtpub.com/authors`.

Customer support

Now that you are the proud owner of a Packt book, we have a number of things to help you to get the most from your purchase.

Downloading the color images of this book

We also provide you with a PDF file that has color images of the screenshots/diagrams used in this book. The color images will help you better understand the changes in the output. You can download this file from `https://www.packtpub.com/sites/default/files/down loads/LearningIoTwithParticlePhotonandElectron_ColorImages.pdf`.

Errata

Although we have taken every care to ensure the accuracy of our content, mistakes do happen. If you find a mistake in one of our books-maybe a mistake in the text or the code-we would be grateful if you could report this to us. By doing so, you can save other readers from frustration and help us improve subsequent versions of this book. If you find any errata, please report them by visiting `http://www.packtpub.com/submit-errata`, selecting your book, clicking on the **Errata Submission Form** link, and entering the details of your errata. Once your errata are verified, your submission will be accepted and the errata will be uploaded to our website or added to any list of existing errata under the Errata section of that title.

To view the previously submitted errata, go to `https://www.packtpub.com/books/conten t/support` and enter the name of the book in the search field. The required information will appear under the **Errata** section.

Piracy

Piracy of copyrighted material on the Internet is an ongoing problem across all media. At Packt, we take the protection of our copyright and licenses very seriously. If you come across any illegal copies of our works in any form on the Internet, please provide us with the location address or website name immediately so that we can pursue a remedy.

Please contact us at `copyright@packtpub.com` with a link to the suspected pirated material.

We appreciate your help in protecting our authors and our ability to bring you valuable content.

Questions

If you have a problem with any aspect of this book, you can contact us at `questions@packtpub.com`, and we will do our best to address the problem.

1

Introducing IoT with Particle Photon and Electron

The Wikipedia page on the **Internet of Things (IoT)** says the following:

> *"The Internet of Things (IoT, sometimes Internet of Everything) is the network of physical objects or "things" embedded with electronics, software, sensors, and connectivity to enable objects to exchange data with the manufacturer, operator and/or other connected devices based on the infrastructure of International Telecommunication Union's Global Standards Initiative."*

This chapter starts with a brief walkthrough of the evolution of the IoT followed by an overview of the basics of IoT-related software and hardware, which every IoT enthusiast should know. The discussion then moves on to introduce Particle, an IoT company (`https://www.particle.io/`), followed by a description of Particle's popular IoT products—Core, Photon, and Electron.

This chapter is divided into the following sections:

- Evolution of the IoT
- Hardware and software in the IoT ecosystem
- Market survey of IoT development boards and cloud services
- What is Particle?
- Photon, Electron, and Core

Evolution of the IoT

It is not very clear exactly who coined the term IoT. Kevin Ashton (`https://en.wikipedia.org/wiki/Kevin_Ashton`) supposedly coined the phrase *Internet of Things* while working for **Procter & Gamble (P&G)** in 1999. Kevin was then working on an RFID (`https://en.wikipedia.org/wiki/Radio-frequency_identification`) initiative by P&G, and proposed taking the system online to the Internet.

In 2005, UN's **International Telecommunications Union (ITU)** (`http://www.itu.int/`), published its first report on IoT. In 2008, the global non-profit organization IPSO Alliance (`http://www.ipso-alliance.org/`) was launched to serve the various communities seeking to establish the IoT by providing coordinated marketing efforts available to the general public. IPSO currently has more than 50 member companies including Google, Cisco, Intel, Texas Instruments, Bosch, Atmel. In 2012, **IoT Consortium (IoTC)** – `http://iofthings.org/`, was founded to educate technology firms, retailers, insurance companies, marketers, media companies, and the wider business community about the value of IoT. IoTC has more than 60 member companies in the area of hardware, software, and analytics, a few of them being Logitech, Node, and **SigFox**.

A 2014 Forbes article by Gil Press says the following:

> *"Gartner estimates that IoT product and service suppliers will generate incremental revenue exceeding $300 billion in 2020. IDC forecasts that the worldwide market for IoT solutions will grow from $1.9 trillion in 2013 to $7.1 trillion in 2020".*

Why the IoT has become a household word now

The IoT has, in recent years, become quite popular and an everyday phenomenon, primarily due to IoT-related hardware, software, accessories, sensors, and Internet connections becoming very affordable and user friendly. An explosion in the availability of free **Integrated Development Environments (IDEs)** and **Software Development Kits (SDKs)** have made programming and deployment of the IoT really simple and easy. Thus, IoT enthusiasts range from school kids, hobbyists, and non-programmers to embedded software engineers specialized in this area.

Hardware and software in the IoT ecosystem

Advancement in technology and affordability has made acquisition and usage of IoT devices very simple. However, in order to decide which IoT package (boards, accessories, sensors, and software) to choose for a particular application, and actually building projects, it is essential to have knowledge of IoT terminology, hardware, and software. In this section, we will introduce you to the essential terminology used when dealing with the IoT. This will also help you to understand and appreciate the features of the Particle IoT products—Core, Photon, and Electron—explained in detail later in the chapter.

Essential terminology

Let's learn about a few terms that we're going to be hearing all throughout this book, and whenever we work with IoT hardware and software components:

Term	Definition
IoT Development Board	A development board is essentially a programmable circuit board which wraps an IoT device. The IoT device's processor/microcontroller, memory, communications ports, input-output pins, sensors, Wi-Fi module, and so on are exposed by the development board, in a convenient way, to the user. A board manufacturer usually provides an IDE with it to write and deploy code to the physical board. A development board with the IDE enables rapid prototyping of IoT projects.
Microcontroller	A microcontroller is a highly compact single **Integrated Circuit** (**IC**) with a processor and limited **Random Access Memory** (**RAM**) and **Read Only Memory** (**ROM**) embedded in it with programmable peripherals. Microcontrollers are computers on a single chip. Because of its limited memory and architecture constraints, usually only one specific program is deployable and runnable on a microcontroller at one time. Preprogrammed microcontrollers are used in electrical machinery such as washing machines, dish-washers, microwave, and so on.
Microprocessor	A microprocessor is a single integrated chip which in itself is a **Central Processing Unit** (**CPU**). The microprocessor has separate RAM and ROM modules, and digital inputs and outputs. The Microprocessor CPU is usually more powerful than that of a microcontroller, and there is provision to add larger amounts of memory externally. This makes microprocessors suitable for general-purpose programming, and are used in desktop computers, laptops, and the like.
Flash Memory	Flash memory is an electronic non-volatile storage device, for example, USB pen-drives, memory cards, and so on. Data in flash memory can be erased and rewritten. Unlike RAM, access speed is lower for flash memories, and also unlike RAM, the data stored in flash memory is not erased when power is switched off. Flash memories are generally used as reusable extra storage.

RTOS	As the name suggests, **real-time operating system** (**RTOS**) responds to events in real time. This means, as soon as an event occurs, a response is guaranteed within an acceptable and calculable amount of time. RTOS can be hard, firm, or soft depending on the amount of flexibility allowed in missing a task deadline. RTOS is essential in embedded systems, where real-time responses are necessary.
M2M	**Machine-to-Machine** (**M2M**) communication encompasses communication between two or more machines (devices, computers, sensors, and so on) over a network (wireless/wired). Basically, it's a variant of the IoT, where things are machines.
Cloud Technology	Cloud refers to computing resources available for use over a network (usually, the Internet). An end user can use such a resource on demand without having to install anything more than a lightweight client in the local machine. The major resources relevant to IoT include data storage, data analytics, data streaming, and communication with other devices.
mBaaS	**Mobile Backend as a Service** (**mBaaS**) is an infrastructure that provides cloud storage, data streaming, push notifications, and other related services for mobile application developers (web, native, IoT app development). The services are exposed via web-based APIs. BaaS is usually provided as a pay-per-use service.
GPIO	**General Purpose Input Output** (**GPIO**) are electrical terminals or pins exposed from ICs and IoT devices/boards that can be used to either send a signal to the device from the outside (input mode), or get a signal out from the inside of the device (output mode). Input or Output mode can be configured by the user at runtime.
Module	Unit of electronics, sometimes a single IC and at other times a group of components that may include ICs, providing a logical function to the device/board. For example, a Wi-Fi module provides Wi-Fi functionality to a board. Other examples are Bluetooth, Ethernet, and USB.
Port	An electrical or radio frequency-based interface available on a board through which external components can communicate with the board. For example, HDMI, USB, Ethernet, 3.5mm jack, and UART (`https://en.wiki pedia.org/wiki/Universal_asynchronous_receiver/transmitter`).

Table 1: Terminology

Network protocols

Connected smart devices need to communicate with each other and exchange large volumes of messages between themselves and the cloud. To ensure near real-time response, smart bandwidth usage, and energy savings on the resource-constrained IoT devices, new protocols have been added to the traditional seven-layer network model (OSI model: `https://en.wikipedia.org/wiki/OSI_model`). The following table shows the major OSI network protocols and the IoT network protocols suitable for various smart, connected devices.

Layer	Examples of traditional network protocols (OSI)	Examples of IoT network protocols
Application, Presentation, Session	HTTP, FTP, SMTP, TLS, RPC, JSON, CSS, GIF, XML	CoAP, MQTT, DDS, M2M service layer
Transport	TCP, UDP	UDP, DTLS
Network	ICMP, IPsec, IPv4, IPv6	6LoWPAN, RPL (Zigbee)
Data Link	IEEE 802.2, L2TP, LLDP, MAC, PPP	IEEE 802.15.4, BLE4.0, RFID, NFC, Cellular
Physical	DSL, Ethernet physical layer, RS-232, any physical transmission medium (for example, Cables)	Wires, sensor drivers to read from sensor devices

Table 2: Layerwise Network Protocols – OSI versus IoT

Market survey of IoT development boards and cloud services

Here we list some of the most popular IoT boards and cloud services, available in the market at the time of writing this book, with some of their important specifications and features. These tables should help you to get an idea as to where Particle products fit in on the IoT map.

IoT development boards

The next table lists the main specifications of popular IoT boards. These specifications are the basic details one has to consider while selecting a board—its specifications in terms of processor and speed, memory, available communication modules and ports, and IO pins. Also, while selecting a board, one has to analyze and match the project's requirements with the available boards, so that the right board is selected for the application in terms of fitment and performance.

Board Name	Microcontroller	Microprocessor	Memory	Modules	Ports	IO Pins
Raspberry Pi 1/2/3	Broadcom SoC BCM2835/6/7	Single/Quad-core ARM 11/Cortex-A7/A53 CPU, VideoCore IV GPU	256 MB/512 MB/1 GB RAM	Ethernet, Wi-Fi, Serial UART, I2C	HDMI, USB, Ethernet (RJ45), GPIO	26/40/40
Arduino Mini	ATmega328	NA	32 KB Flash 2 KB SRAM	NA	NA	14
Arduino Yun	ATmega32u4	Atheros AR9331	32 KB Flash 2.5 KB SRAM, 16 MB Flash, 64 MB RAM	Wi-Fi, Ethernet	USB, Ethernet (RJ45)	20
Intel Edison	MCU at 100 MHz (Intel Atom Soc)	Dual-core CPU at 500 MHz (Intel Atom Soc)	4 GB Flash, 1 GB RAM	Wi-Fi, Bluetooth 4.0	USB, UART, SPI, GPIO	28
Libelium Waspmote	ATmega1281	NA	128 KB Flash, 8 KB SRAM	Temp, humidity, light sensors, (optional) GPS	UART, I2C, SPI, USB	19

NodeMCU ESP8266	ESP 8266 SoC	ESP-12 module	4 MB Flash	Wi-Fi, Serial UART, ADC	UART, GPIO, SPI	14
BeagleBone Black	Sitara SoC AM3358/9	AM335x 1 GHz ARM Cortex-A8	512 MB RAM, 2/4 GB flash storage	Ethernet, Serial UART, ADC, I2C	Ethernet (RJ45), HDMI, USB, GPIO	24
CubieBoard	ARM Cortex-A8 CPU	AllWinner A10 SoC	512 MB/ 1 GB RAM, 4 GB flash memory	Ethernet, Serial UART, ADC, I2C	Ethernet (RJ45), USB, SATA	96

Table 3: IoT development boards

Cloud services (PaaS, BaaS, M2M)

It is important to know what kind of cloud service we will be dealing with, and whether our board has open standards and allows us to use our own personal service easily, or whether the board-provided service needs some manipulation to use in the current project.

Cloud service name	Salient features
Amazon Web Services (https://aws.amazon.com/) Microsoft Azure (https://azure.microsoft.com/) Cloud Foundry (https://www.cloudfoundry.org/) IBM Bluemix (http://www.ibm.com/cloud-computing/bluemix/)	**Platform as a Service (PaaS)** provides **virtual machine (VM)**, storage, application services, deployment and management, mobile and device services, and big data analytics.

Parse (http://www.parse.com/) Kinvey (http://www.kinvey.com/) AnyPresence (http://www.anypresence.com/) Appcelerator (http://www.appcelerator.com/)	mBaaS provides ways to link mobile apps to backend cloud storage, user management, push notifications, and integration with social networking services.
ThingWorx (https://www.thingworx.com/)	M2M offering from PTC (http://www.ptc.com/)

Table 4: Cloud services

What is Particle?

Particle (https://www.particle.io), formerly known as Spark, is a company started by Zach Supalla. It provides hardware and software for the development of IoT projects.

The journey of Particle

The first company started by Zach Supalla in 2011 was known as Hex Goods, and it sold designer products online. In early 2012, Hex Goods was shut down, and Zach started a second company called Switch Devices, which dealt with connected lighting. Switch Devices was then renamed Spark Devices. The name Spark was used as it provided a double meaning to the founders. Spark stood for spark of light and also sparks of inspiration.

In early 2013, Spark transformed to an IoT platform for engineers and developers. The name Spark also did not last long as the founders felt Spark created confusion for a lot of users. There exist 681 live trademarks that include the word Spark. Apart from the number of trademarks, there are some other great, unrelated software and hardware products employing the name Spark in them—some of them being Apache Spark, SparkFun, and Spark NZ. It has been reported that a lot of people logged on to Zach's #spark IRC channel and asked questions about big data.

The name Particle was finally chosen, as it gave plenty of room to grow in terms of products and offerings. Particle, in scientific terms, is a single discreet unit within a larger system. The name draws a parallel with the mission of Particle—the company which provides development kits and devices as single units used to build the greater whole of IoT.

We'll cover Particle IoT products in depth, and see how and when they perform better than other IoT development boards.

Why Particle?

Today, the most recurring problem with all existing IoT prototyping boards is that of connectivity. In order to connect the existing boards to the Internet, additional components such as Wi-Fi or GSM modules have to be attached in the development environment as well as in production. Attaching external devices for communication is cumbersome, and adds another point of failure with frequent issues such as Internet unavailability, intermittent network connectivity, and so on. This leads to a bad experience for the developer.

Developers have to frequently (re)write code, deploy it onto the device(s), test, debug, fix any bugs, rinse, and repeat. The problem with code deployment with existing boards is that the boards need to be connected to a computer, which means for even the smallest code update, the device/board needs to be connected to the developer's computer, either by moving the computer to the device (which may be located at a not-so-easily accessible location) or vice versa. This poses a problem when the device, after an update at the developer's site, has to be placed back in its original production environment for testing and debugging the new changes. This means large turnaround times to load new code into production.

Particle provides products that have built-in Wi-Fi modules or GSM modules, which help in easy connection to a network or the Internet, with support for **Over-The-Air (OTA)** code deployment. This removes the hassle of adding extra modules on the prototyping boards for connectivity, and it also allows pushing code or testing/debugging onsite. As previously mentioned, one of the important features that differentiates Particle products from other devices is the Particle device's ability of deploying code over the air. New code can be deployed onto the device or **burnt**, as the process is called in embedded systems parlance, via REST API calls, which makes it very convenient to provide updates. This feature of Particle products helps with a faster code release cycle and testing/debugging.

What does Particle offer?

Particle offers a suite of hardware and software tools to help prototype, scale, and manage the IoT products. It also provides the ability to build cloud-connected IoT prototypes quickly. If you're satisfied with your prototype and want to productize your IoT design, no problem there. It helps us to go from a single prototype to millions of units with a cloud platform that can scale as the number of devices grow.

The popular Particle hardware devices are listed as follows:

- **Core**: A tiny Wi-Fi development kit for prototyping and scaling your IoT product. Reprogrammable and connected to the cloud, this has now been superseded by the Photon.
- **Photon**: A tiny Wi-Fi development kit for prototyping and scaling your IoT product. Reprogrammable and connected to the cloud.
- **Electron**: A tiny development kit for creating 2G/3G cellular connected products.

The Photon and the Core are bundled with Wi-Fi modules, which help them connect to a network or the Internet without adding any extra modules.

The Electron has a 3G/2G GSM module, that can be used to send or receive messages directly or connect to the Internet.

The firmware for the Photon, Electron, and Core can be written in a web-based IDE provided by Particle, and the deployment of the firmware code to the device is done over the air. Particle also offers SDKs for mobile and the Web to extend the IoT experience from the devices/sensors to the phone and the Web.

A detailed comparison between Photon, Electron, and Core is given in the next section.

Photon, Electron, and Core

The first prototyping board that was released by Particle (then known as Spark) was called Core. The subsequent prototyping boards released by Particle were called Photon and Electron. Core was superseded by the more powerful, faster, and less expensive Photon. Sale of Core has since been discontinued at Particle's online store at `https://store.particle.io/`, and hence, we will primarily discuss the Photon and the Electron. At the end of this chapter, we do a feature-wise comparison of the boards. The comparison can help one arrive at the most suitable board for one's project needs.

Spark Core

The Spark Core was the first IoT prototyping board released by Spark (now known as Particle) in a successful Kickstarter campaign that raised $567,968 from 5,549 backers. The Spark Core is an Arduino-compatible, Wi-Fi enabled, cloud-powered development platform that makes creating Internet-connected hardware a breeze.

Figure 1: Spark Core

The technical details of Spark Core are as follows:

- ARM Cortex M3 CPU
- 72 MHz operating frequency
- 128 KB flash memory
- 20 KB RAM
- 12-bit ADC
- Wireless programming
- Analogue and digital I/O pins
- TI CC3000 Wi-Fi module
- 802.11 b/g Wi-Fi support
- USB 2.0 full-speed interface

The Spark Core is priced at $39 USD.

Particle Photon

The Photon was built considering the feedback received from Core users. Thus, the Photon is the successor of the Core, and is more powerful than the Core in terms of CPU and memory.

The Photon can be ordered with or without headers, which means it has the flexibility to be used as a prototyping board (with headers) by hobbyists, or it can be soldered into a bigger circuit (without headers) for production.

The Photon is also Arduino-compatible, like its predecessor.

Figure 2: Particle Photon

The technical details of the Photon are as follows:

- 120 Mhz ARM Cortex M3 processor
- Wireless programming
- Broadcom BCM43362 Wi-Fi chip
- Supports 802.11 b/g/n Wi-Fi
- 1 MB flash memory
- 128 KB RAM
- 18 GPIO and peripheral pins
- On-board RGB LED
- Real-time operating system (FreeRTOS)

- Support for **AP** (**Access Point**) mode (SoftAP)
- Open source design
- FCC, CE, and IC certified

The Photon has additional capabilities such as a wake-up pin for waking up from low power modes. The Photon is optimized to use less power, and this is made possible by the new Wi-Fi module it uses—Broadcom's BCM43362, which it incorporates. This new Wi-Fi chip powers other popular IoT products such as Nest Protect, LIFX, and others, as it provides the most stable solution. The Photon is available for $19 USD, and can be purchased from Particle's online store at `https://store.particle.io`.

Particle Electron

The Electron is a cousin of the Photon with minor differences. It has a GSM module instead of a Wi-Fi module. The Electron can be used for creating cellular-connected electronics projects and products. It ships with a SIM card, and is optimized for low-bandwidth messages. The SIM card offers affordable data plans for over 100 countries worldwide through carriers such as Telefonica, AT&T, T-Mobile, O2, Movistar, Vivo, Telenor, Rogers, and many more. You can find the list of countries where the Electron's GSM connectivity is available at `https://www.particle.io/cellular`.

Figure 3: Particle Electron

The technical details of the Electron are as follows:

- 1 MB flash
- 128 KB RAM
- Wireless programming
- U-blox SARA-U260/U270 (3G) and G350 (2G) cellular module
- STM32F205 120 MHz ARM Cortex M3 microcontroller
- RGB status LED
- 30 mixed-signal GPIO and advanced peripherals
- Open source design
- RTOS
- FCC, CE, and IC certified

The Electron is available both in 2G and 3G variants. The Electron 2G is available for US $39, while the Electron the 3G variant is available for US $59. The Electron SIM card is available without any contracts, and the basic data charges are $2.99 per month for 1 MB and an additional $0.99 for each additional megabyte of data transferred.

Comparison

This section provides a tabular comparison between Spark Core, Particle Photon, and Particle Electron. This table can help in an easy reference of technical specifications, and can also help decide the best board to use for a given project.

Feature	Spark Core	Particle Photon	Particle Electron
Wi-Fi Support	802.11 b/g	802.11 b/g/n	No
Wireless Module	TI CC3000	Broadcom BCM43362	U-Blox SARA U-Series or G-Series
Microcontroller	STM32F103	STM32F205	STM32F205
CPU speed	72 MHz	120 MHz	120 Mhz
Flash memory	128 KB	1 MB	1 MB
RAM	20 KB	128 KB	128 KB
Wakeup pin exposed	No	Yes	Yes
VBAT pin exposed	No	Yes	Yes
No. of GPIO pins	18	18	30

UART present	Yes	Yes	Yes
JTAG present	Yes	Yes	Yes
I2C present	Yes	Yes	Yes
SPI present	Yes	Yes	Yes
ADC present	Yes	Yes	Yes
DAC present	No	Yes	Yes
CAN present	No	Yes	Yes
Dimensions and weight	35.6 mm x 20.3 mm x 11 mm, 6 g	With headers -36.6 mm x 20.3 mm x 6.9 mm, 5 g Without headers – 36.6 mm x 20.3 mm x 4.3 mm, 3.7 g	20.32 mm x 16.5 mm x 52.1 mm, 10 g
Operating voltage and current	3.6V to 6V, ~ 50 mA to 300 mA normally, 3.2 µA in deep sleep	3.6V to 5.5V, ~ 80 mA normally ~ 80 uA in deep sleep mode	3.7V, ~ 180 mA normally ~ 130 uA in deep sleep mode.
Price	$39	$19	$39 or $59

Table 5: Comparison of Particle products

Summary

In this chapter, we learnt about the IoT, and how it all began. We briefly touched upon major organizations involved in the IoT, common terminology used, and we looked at different hardware products and cloud services we have available for building IoT projects. Further, we saw how Particle fits into the IoT picture, and the different products it has on offer for us to make the most of.

In the next chapter, we'll get hands-on, and learn to set up the IoT kits for our projects.

2

Fire Up Your Kit

In this chapter, you are going to build a Twitter and e-mail interaction application. The Twitter and e-mail project aims to give you hands-on experience with the Photon board, Particle cloud, and writing code using **ParticleJS** (https://docs.particle.io/reference/javascript/), a library to interact with Particle devices and the Particle cloud. We'll start the chapter with a brief list of the essential features of **FreeRTOS** (http://www.freertos.org/), the Photon's operating system. This will help you understand the functionalities in this project, and to troubleshoot unexpected behaviors. This is followed by detailed steps for setting up the Photon and the **Internet Button** to communicate with Twitter and send an e-mail.

The list of topics covered in this chapter are as follows:

- Essentials of FreeRTOS and hardware resources
- Flow diagram for the Twitter project
- Getting the Photon online
- Twitter and e-mail interaction project
- Troubleshooting

To build the Twitter and e-mail project, we will be using a Photon/Core with Particle's Internet Button. The Internet Button (`https://www.particle.io/button`) is a small, circular accessory board from Particle. It has directional buttons, LED indicators, and an accelerometer. In conjunction with a Photon or Core, it can be used to perform actions on the Internet by pushing its buttons or sensing motion. Its LEDs can be used to notify us of events such as the state of a switch, motion detection, new e-mail in your inbox, and so on.

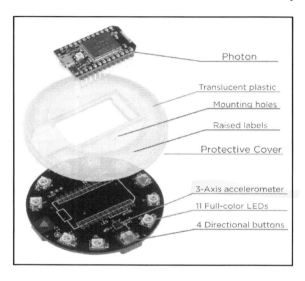

Figure 1: Particle Internet Button

Essentials of FreeRTOS and hardware resources

During the process of building the Twitter project, you may be baffled by some unexpected behavior of your program. It is easy to debug these anomalies if you understand some basics of how the operating system/firmware works. This knowledge will also help you effectively use the programming language and library features to write perfectly working code.

In *Essential terminology*, Chapter 1, *Introducing IoT with Particle Photon and Electron*, we briefly mentioned that RTOS responds to events in real time, and is used in embedded systems. Real-time responses, along with its small memory and energy footprint, has made FreeRTOS a very popular choice for many other embedded chips as well. One of the major improvements in the Photon is that using FreeRTOS, the system code and application code now run in separate threads without compromising the efficiency of real-time responses. The user's application code is usually very small (a few KBs), but the system code is bulkier. In the Core, over-the-air program updates are slow, because both system and application code have to be bundled together. In the Photon, during program updates from the cloud, only the small user code is transferred, as the system code is written only once, that is, the first time the firmware program is written.

Event handling is very strict in any RTOS to ensure a real-time response. The RTOS's highest priority is to process and finish a task as fast as possible to generate a response at the earliest; hence, the interrupts (https://en.wikipedia.org/wiki/Interrupt), which are signals to tell the processor that an event needs immediate attention, have very short lives during which the RTOS blocks the running tasks, and takes up the new urgent task for execution. Sometimes, when an interrupt is fired, the OS may already be running some blocking, higher-priority task, thus ignoring the new interrupt. This means a new interrupt can die before even informing the OS of the new task. How does this affect you? Sometimes, you may observe that your code to turn on an LED got executed, but the LED never lit up! This means, the interrupt to turn on the LED was never able to speak to the processor/OS on time. How can you fix this issue? One way to work around this issue is to keep executing the "turn on LED" code in a loop for a few iterations, preferably with a small delay between iterations, and one of the interrupts is very likely to reach its goal for sure! There is no harm done if more than one LED glow request reaches the OS. You can handle most of the LEDs and sensors attached to your board this way if you find that the sensor is not being reliably read, or the LED is not behaving as expected.

In the Photon, around 128 KB of RAM is allocated for user code. Although this is a huge upgrade from the Core, which has around 20 KB of RAM for user code, 128 KB is still very lean; hence, the programmer needs to respect this in his/her program.

How does this affect you? If you keep sending HTTP requests continuously to the Photon, the program running on the Photon may stop responding after a while. This is because each HTTP request takes up a chunk of memory while it is being processed, and frequent requests can eat up all of the user memory. This can crash your program. The RTOS has some role to play here too. Another problem that could cause a program crash is memory fragmentation. This means that although there is free memory, there is no contiguous free memory equal to or greater than the amount that has been requested by the code; hence, even if there is free memory, out-of-memory exceptions can occur. The workaround for the HTTP issue is to reduce the frequency of the messages by adding some delay in the code execution loop so that frequent requests are ignored, and requests are processed at a manageable pace. A good thing is that the Photon uses LED flash codes to inform the programmer of any code crash (for example, the LED blinking red several times). This is an effective debugging tool.

For the Twitter project, we will keep the board powered up with a USB cable attached to the PC; hence, we don't need a separate power source for the board during coding and development. But in most real-life projects, including the later projects in this book, we will be powering up the board with batteries instead of a PC, laptop, or a wall wart. However, batteries don't last long; hence, the programmer is expected to be careful in saving battery power as much as possible. How can one achieve that? The programmer should reduce the frequency of high-energy activities (for example, usage of Bluetooth and Wi-Fi Radio). In later chapters, we will illustrate how you can smartly put the board to sleep in between high-energy activities so that you can get a significant lifetime extension on the battery.

There are several other hardware/software features you need to be aware of while using boards such as the Photon and the Electron. We have restricted the discussion here to the areas that can affect the LED glow and HTTP request behaviors, as these are what you will be working with in the Twitter project. In the following chapters, we will get to know more about the critical hardware and software internals, which will help us create robust applications.

Flow diagram for the Twitter project

The following diagram depicts the connectivity and data flow between various components of the Twitter project, and the process involved in setting up the same.

The process begins with—**Photon-Internet Button** pair connected to the computer via USB. Next, the **Photon** is registered with the **Particle cloud**. Now, we're ready to write and deploy code using the Web IDE, and setup Twitter and email authentication. Finally the Photon is ready to communicate with Twitter and send email using Webhooks over the Wi-Fi network.

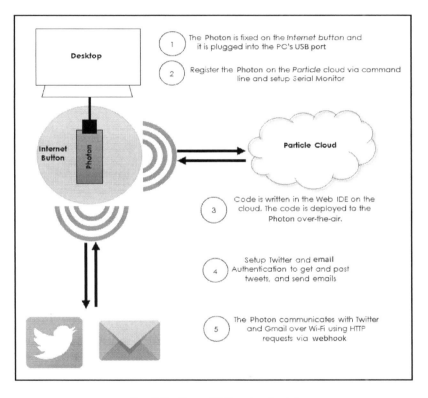

Figure 2: Flow diagram of Twitter and email project

Getting the Photon online

The Particle Photon and Core have built-in Wi-Fi modules, a Microcontroller, I/O Pins, Buttons, and LEDs. You will be using the Photon's buttons to configure the modes of operation of the Photon and Core.

If you hold the Photon or Core board such that the USB connector is at the top and the buttons are facing you, then the **Mode/Setup Button** is the one on the left, and the Reset Button is to the right. If you look closely, these buttons are also labelled right on the board, as shown in the following image:

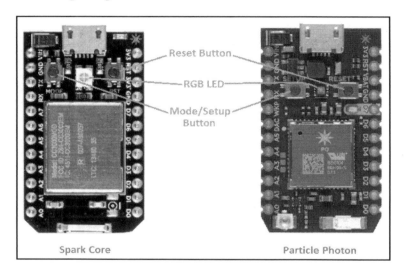

Figure 3: Spark Core and Particle Photon

The **RGB LED** is in the center of the Photon and Core, between the **Mode/Setup** and **Reset** buttons. The color of the **RGB LED** determines the current mode of operation. All the color codes are explained at this link: `https://docs.particle.io/support/troubleshooting/troubleshooting-support/photon/`.

Setting up the Photon or Core

The Photon and Core boards can be set up and used with an iPhone or Android application as well as by using a command-line tool provided by Particle.

For example, the *Particle* app on Google Play Store, available at `https://play.google.com/store/apps/details?id=io.particle.android.app`, allows you to play with the Photon without writing any code. More details on using the Particle mobile apps are available at `https://docs.particle.io/guide/getting-started/tinker/photon/`.

In this book, we will demonstrate the use of Particle **Command Line Interface (CLI)** tools to set up your Photon or Core.

If you have not already created a Particle account at `https://build.particle.io`, go ahead and do so now. Make sure you keep a note of the e-mail ID and password you use to sign up for your Particle account. These credentials are required when you use the CLI to log in and add a board to your account.

Software and hardware requirements

You will require the following hardware and software to set up the board:

- **Hardware**
    - Particle device (Photon or Core)
    - USB cable
    - Computer with Internet connection
- **Software**
    - Linux or Windows operating system
    - Node.js (`https://www.nodejs.org`)
    - Particle CLI (`https://docs.particle.io/guide/tools-and-features/cli/photon/`)
    - Particle Driver—only required if you are using Windows OS

Software setup

Node.js is a **Runtime Environment** that allows running JavaScript programs on the command line. Head over to `https://www.nodejs.org`, and download the correct binary installable file depending on the operating system you use. Node JS is available for Mac OS, Windows, and Linux operating systems.

Node.js has a bundled package (library) and dependency manager called **Node Package Manager (npm)**. This is used to install publicly available Node.js libraries.

Particle provides its CLI tools in the form of a publicly available, open source Node.js library called `particle-cli`. This library, upon installation on your computer, makes a command-line tool called particle available to you.

To install the particle CLI, open up a terminal or command window on your computer. Make sure your computer has Internet access. At the command prompt, run the following `npm install` command:

Particle CLI installation command for Linux:

```
# npm install -g particle-cli
```

Particle-CLI installation command for Windows:
```
D:\> npm install -g particle-cli
```

Note that this preceding command is for a software installation that needs admin privileges; hence, it requires the user to be logged in as root, the superuser, or admin, on Linux. The # prompt signifies that the terminal was run by the root user. A regular user's terminal prompt would be $.

Going forward, we'll list only the Linux version of the commands for brevity. When dealing with Particle CLI, the Windows commands are identical to the Linux commands, unless stated otherwise.

This command installs the Node.js package named `particle-cli` on the computer. The package is installed globally (note the `-g` option in the command), so any user can access it from any directory. The command should print the progress of installation and exit without any errors.

Windows users will additionally need to install the Particle Driver for Windows available at `https://s3.amazonaws.com/spark-website/Spark.zip`.

To install the driver, go to the Windows **Device Manager** (found by typing **device manager** in the search bar of the Start menu), and right-click on your Particle device under the **Other Devices** node (on Windows 10, this should appear under the **Ports** node) to open a Context menu as shown in the next screenshot. Click on **Update Driver Software...**, browse, and select the driver software on your computer wherever you unzipped the drivers. The driver is called `spark_core.cat`.

For more information, see `https://docs.particle.io/guide/getting-started/connect/photon/`, and look for the section *Installing the Particle driver.*

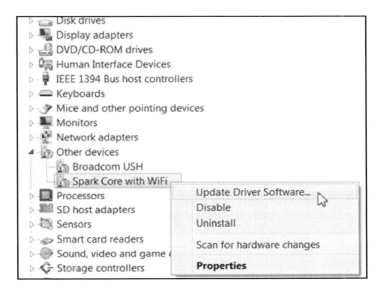

Figure 4: Windows Device Manager

Connecting Particle Photon or Core

Connect the Particle Photon or Core to your computer using a USB cable. The board should be in listening mode. This is indicated by the onboard RGB LED blinking blue. In case the board is not in listening mode, press the Mode Button for more than three seconds until the device is in listening mode (that is, LED blinking blue).

At the command prompt, run the following particle setup command:

```
$ particle setup
```

The setup proceeds like a wizard, asking you a series of questions including your Particle account details, at which point you need to provide the e-mail ID and password you used to sign up at https://build.particle.io.

The setup will identify your board connected through USB, and will also scan for Wi-Fi networks available in your vicinity. Select your Wi-Fi network, which is identified by the SSID (Wi-Fi network name), and provide the required Wi-Fi security credentials so that your Particle board can connect to the Internet and be claimed—a term used by Particle to mean "add board to my account".

Once the device is claimed, that is, it is connected to the Internet and added to your account, the onboard LED should be "breathing" cyan—a slow blink where the brightness increases and decreases periodically in a slow rhythm, reminiscent of breathing.

The Web IDE

The nice thing about using Particle boards is that it provides a web-based IDE, simply called **Web IDE**. This means there is no software installation required on your local machine for code development. The code that you write in the Web IDE is deployed over the Internet onto the Photon/Core.

The Web IDE is available at https://build.particle.io.

It provides a text area to write code, and options to deploy code on the Photon/Core, as shown in the following screenshot:

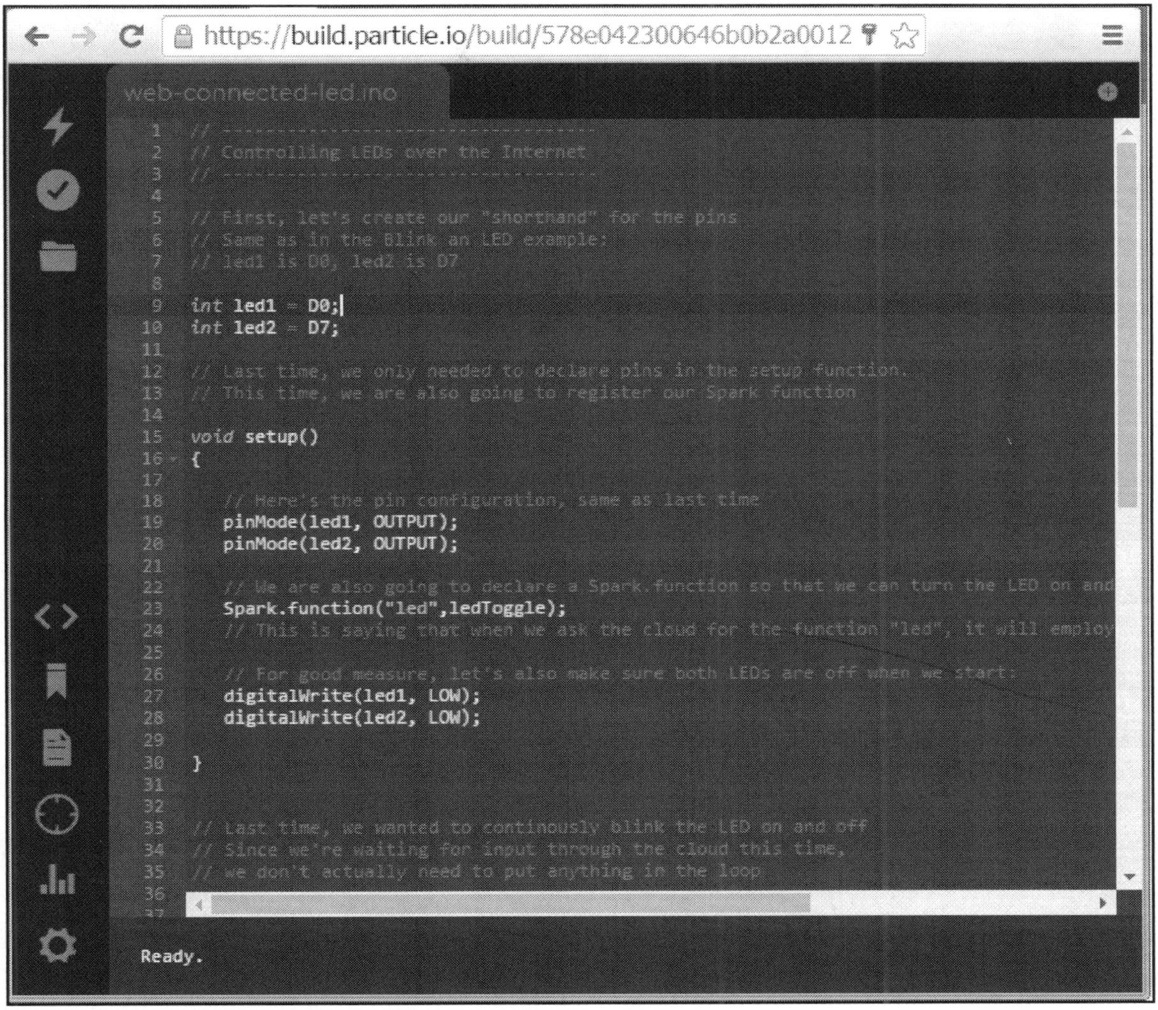

Figure 5: Particle Web IDE

It also provides a way to explore libraries submitted by other users, or develop your own and use them with just a few clicks.

Clicking the Flash button ⚡ at the top-left corner of the Web IDE verifies the code, compiles the current code, generates the corresponding binary format, and sends the binary to your claimed device over the air where it is flashed onto the device—all in one go.

You can manage your devices from the **device** tab in the Web IDE. This can be accessed using the Devices button .

Twitter and e-mail interaction project

The aim of the Twitter project is to get you accustomed to the development cycle using Particle Photon or Core. In this project, we will be building a connected application using Particle Photon and the Internet Button. The Internet Button has four programmable physical buttons, eleven RGB LEDs, and a three-axis accelerometer.

The Internet Button, used as an accessory to the Photon and Core, is powered by the Particle board, which fits snugly onto it.

The project that we are building here is quite simple. The idea is to use the Internet Button as a physical notification device as well as an input device, with two different ways to provide input-button press and "shake".

When we are done with this project, a tweet should be posted by shaking the Internet Button. The LEDs on the Internet Button will be turned on when a new tweet is posted this way. On pressing a button on the Internet Button, an e-mail will be sent out to your e-mail ID. On pressing another button, a tweet will be fetched and displayed in the serial console. The Internet Button LEDs will light up as a notification for all events.

Setting up a Twitter developer account

Twitter provides REST APIs to fetch and post data to twitter.com. The Twitter REST APIs can be used only after authentication using OAuth or Bearer Token (`https://en.wikipedia.org/wiki/OAuth`). Head over to `https://dev.twitter.com` and register an application. The name of the application has to be unique. Twitter will then generate the Application Key, Application Secret, OAuth Key, and OAuth Secret, which are to be used when interacting with Twitter APIs.

Sending web requests using Particle webhooks

Webhooks (`https://docs.particle.io/guide/tools-and-hookfeatures/webhooks/`) are a simple way to send/receive data from Particle devices to/from Internet-based services when an event happens. Using webhooks, Particle boards can send HTTP and HTTPS requests upon receiving subscribed events. Twitter and e-mail APIs are based on HTTPS; hence, webhooks are suitable for this project, and we will see how to set them up.

Particle devices have the ability to both `https://docs.particle.io/reference/firmware/photon/#particle-publish-` to the Particle cloud as well as `https://docs.particle.io/reference/firmware/electron/#particle-subscribe-` from the cloud.

A webhook listens for a specific event published by a device. When this event is published (triggered), the webhook makes a `http://rve.org.uk/dumprequest` to a preconfigured Internet URL. The request sent by the webhook by this URL can include information about the event, such as its name as well as any data included when the event was published.

In our case, the web request will be the HTTPS APIs of Twitter and Mailgun, (an e-mail sending service) used to perform the functionalities of this project.

Creating a webhook

Webhooks can be created from the cloud-based Particle Dashboard as well as by using the Particle CLI. You can pass in an `eventName`, `url`, and `deviceID` as arguments to the Particle CLI. You can also create your own custom JSON file that includes webhook parameters, and pass this JSON file as an argument to the Particle CLI. We will use the JSON method, as it is convenient to pass additional data, such as authentication.

The JSON file can be created using any text editor, and it can contain the following data, some of which are optional:

- `event`: Name of the event as referred in the code, which should trigger the webhook
- `url`: The web address that will be invoked when the webhook is triggered
- `access_token`: A string used for authentication
- `requestType`: The type of HTTP(S) request: `GET`, `POST`, `PUT`, or `DELETE`
- `headers`: Any additional HTTP headers that have to be sent in the request—to be provided as key/value pairs
- `query`: Query parameters that are to be sent to the URL—to be provided as key/value pairs

- `auth`: A basic HTTP authentication header, mainly used for OAuth and Bearer Token
- `mydevices`: A Boolean value which is set to true if you want to limit the webhook triggering to devices owned by you

An example of the contents of a `webhook` JSON file is as follows:

```
{
    "eventName": "DataUpdate",
    "url": "https://some.dashboard.com/api/events",
    "requestType": "POST",
    "headers": {
      "Content-Type": "application/json",
    },
    "json": {
      "key": "XXXXXX_data",
      "value": "YYYYYYYYYY"
    },
    "mydevices": true,
    "deviceid": "my device id here"
}
```

Once the `webhook` JSON file is created, you can create the webhook by executing the following command at the command prompt:

```
$ particle webhook create <your-web-hook-file>.json
Using settings from the file <your-web-hook-file>.json
. . .
. . .
. . .
Successfully created webhook with ID 587******************319
$
```

Upon successful creation of the webhook, a unique `webhook ID` is returned, as shown in the preceding code snippet. Some output is suppressed with . . . for clarity.

Listing and deleting webhooks

It may not be possible to mentally keep track of all the webhooks you create; hence, Particle CLI provides a way to view all the webhooks that are present in your account. To view all the webhooks created, run the following command:

```
$ particle webhook list
Found 1 hooks registered
```

```
1.) Hook ID 587******************319 is watching for "DataUpdate"
and sending to: https://some.dashboard.com
for device 390******************031
created at 2016-07-20T11:03:43.598Z
$
```

The webhook IDs can be used to delete webhooks with the following command:

```
$ particle webhook delete <webhook ID>
```

Putting it all together

We have learnt how to make web requests using webhooks, and we have the prerequisites for using the Twitter API. Let's go ahead and build our first application using the knowledge from the sections we've seen so far.

Setting up the Twitter and e-mail webhook

The Twitter webhook has to be created before it can be used in the firmware code on the device. We create a JSON file named `Twitter.json` to create the webhook. Start a new text file in a text editor, and copy the following code into it:

```
{
  "event": "twitterFetch",
  "url": "https://api.twitter.com/1.1/search/tweets.json",
  "requestType": "GET",
  "headers": {
    "Authorization" : "Bearer XXXXXX"
  },
  "query": {
    "q": "{{TWIT_ID}}",
    "count": "1"
  },
  "mydevices": true
}
```

In this preceding file, we create the following:

- The value of `event`, `"twitterFetch"`, is the name of the event that this webhook will respond to.
- The value of `url` is the Twitter URL that fetches tweets. This URL, appended with additional query data, is called by the webhook when the `"twitterFetch"` event happens.

- The value of `requestType` is set to `"GET"` as the Twitter URL happens to be this.
- The value of `Authorization` under `headers` is the **Authorization Bearer Token** for Twitter. This should be generated by signing into the website at `https://dev` `.twitter.com` with your Twitter account. In the file content within the text editor (shown in the previous screenshot), replace the text `"Bearer XXXXX"` with the generated Bearer Token.
- The value of `query` is the additional data that the Twitter URL will need, and that the webhook will append to `url` before invoking the URL.
- The value of `mydevices`, as explained earlier, is set to true so that the webhook responds to only our device's events.

Save the text file with the name `Twitter.json`.

Now the JSON file is ready to be used in the Particle CLI `webhook create` command.

At the command prompt, make sure you are in the directory containing the `Twitter.json` file. Then execute the following command:

```
$ particle webhook create Twitter.json
Using settings from the file Twitter.json
...
...
...
Successfully created webhook with ID 292*****************480
$
```

We will now create another webhook, which will be used for sending an e-mail. We will be using the service provided by **Mailgun** (`http://www.mailgun.com/`) to send an e-mail to your e-mail ID. Mailgun provides REST APIs to send e-mails and it can be used to send up to 300 e-mails per day for free.

Create a JSON file named `Mailgun.json` in a text editor with the following content:

```
{
  "event":"mailgun",
  "url":" https://api.mailgun.net/v3/XXXXXX.mailgun.org/messages",
  "requestType":"POST",
  "auth":{
    "api":"key-XXXXXX"
  },
  "json":{
    "from": "Mailgun Sandbox
    <postmaster@sandboxXXXXXX.mailgun.org>",
    "to": "Your Name <your-email-id>",
    "subject": "New Tweet Received",
```

```
    "text": "You have received a new tweet and this email is being
    sent from Particle Core."
  },
  "mydevices":true
}
```

In this preceding file, `Mailgun.json`, we create the following:

- The value of `event`, `"mailgun"`, is the name of the event that this webhook will respond to.
- The value of `url` is the Mailgun service URL that sends the e-mail. The XXXXXX in the URL will be generated by Mailgun, and displayed to you when you register with Mailgun; this has to be replaced in the JSON file before creating the webhook. This final URL, appended with additional query data, is called by the webhook when the `"mailgun"` event happens.
- The value of `requestType` is set to `"POST"`, as the Mailgun URL happens to be this.
- The value of `api` under `auth` is the API Key necessary to use the Mailgun service. This API Key will be generated by Mailgun, and displayed to you when you register with it. `"key-XXXXXX"` has to be replaced with the generated API Key in the JSON file before creating the webhook.
- The value of `json` is the data that the Mailgun service URL will need, and that the webhook will post to `url` while invoking the URL. This is where you specify the `from` address, `to` address, `subject`, and body (`text`) of the e-mail that you wish to receive. You should replace the placeholders appropriately.
- The value of `mydevices`, as explained earlier, is set to `true` so that the webhook responds to only our device's events.

Save the text file with the name `Mailgun.json`.

Now the JSON file is ready to be used in the Particle CLI `webhook create` command.

At the command prompt, make sure you are in the directory containing the `Mailgun.json` file. Then execute the following command:

```
$ particle webhook create Mailgun.json
Using settings from the file Mailgun.json
...
...
...
Successfully created webhook with ID 564******************381
$
```

How to sense motion?

The Internet Button has a built-in three-axis accelerometer, which can be used to detect and measure movement and orientation (of the Internet Button). As part of this project, we want to send a random tweet when the Internet Button is shaken. The Internet Button can sense and output changes in acceleration along the X, Y, and Z– axes. This can be used to sense movement or a "shake".

We will use the following firmware code for sensing movement using the Internet Button's accelerometer readings, and then turn on some LEDs.

In all the code listings, entries prefixed with // are code comments, which explain the code below it. The comments do not affect the working of the code.

Go to Particle Build (Web IDE), and create a new application. Type in or copy the following code into the Web IDE's editor:

```
// Program: Shake to Light Up
// ---------------------------------------------------

//The header file to manage the Internet Button
#include "SparkButton/SparkButton.h"

//Header file for using abs() function
#include "math.h"

// Create the SparkButton object using which we will
// manage the Internet Button
SparkButton button = SparkButton();

// Variables to store the current value of acceleration
// along X,Y and Z-Axes
int currentX, currentY, currentZ;

// Variables to store the previous values of acceleration
// along X,Y and Z-Axes
int previousX, previousY, previousZ;

// The minimum change in acceleration that will trigger an event
int motionThreshold;

// The code in the setup() function runs once when the device is
// powered on or reset. Used for setting up states, modes, etc
void setup(){

  // Start the Internet Button
```

```
  button.begin();
  // Get the initial values of acceleration along the X,Y and
  // Z-Axes. These values will be in the range -128 to +127
  previousX = button.readX();
  previousY = button.readY();
  previousZ = button.readZ();

  // Set the motionThreshold to a value which will be reached
  // only if the Internet Button is shaken. The value of 50
  // Worked nicely in our setup. You can tweak this value for
  // best results.
  motionThreshold = 50;
}
```

We've so far included the needed libraries, declared the necessary variables, and defined the setup function, which runs once, initializing some variables, as soon as the device is powered on. We will now write code where most of the action happens: the loop function.

```
// The loop() function, in contrast to setup(), runs all the time,
// over and over again. In this loop, we periodically
// check for change in acceleration and take appropriate action
void loop(){
  // Read the current value of acceleration along X,Y and Z-Axes
  currentX = button.readX();
  currentY = button.readY();
  currentZ = button.readZ();
  // Check if the Internet Button has accelerated by more than
  // the motionThreshold from the previous value, along any of
  // the three axes
  if (abs(currentX - previousX) > motionThreshold ||
      abs(currentY - previousY) > motionThreshold ||
      abs(currentZ - previousZ) > motionThreshold) {

        // In case there was a movement, all LEDs are made to glow
        // white for 2 seconds.
        // The format here is allLedsOn(red, green, blue), where
        // red, green, and blue are brightness values each ranging
        // from 0-255, 0 is off and 255 is the brightest.
        // Here, we're making a color with ALL the red, green, and
        // blue - which is White
        button.allLedsOn(255, 255, 255);
        // Wait 2000 milliseconds (2 seconds)
        delay(2000);
        // Turn off all the LEDs
        button.allLedsOff();
    }
  // set the current values as the previous ones, getting
  // ready for the next iteration
```

```
    previousX = currentX;
    previousY = currentY;
    previousZ = currentZ;
}
```

This completes our first program. You should be able to flash it to your device from the Web IDE, and test the program by shaking your Internet Button!

Sensing button presses – programming the buttons

The Internet Button has four programmable buttons; that is, pressing each button can be made to trigger a different event. In the following example, we will program the device to light up the Internet Button's LEDs when some of its buttons are pressed. The code for doing this is given in the following listing. Here, we've removed the comments for lines of code that have already been explained in the previous listing, for brevity.

In the Web IDE, create a new application. Type in or copy the following code into the Web IDE's editor. This program sense button presses and turn on LEDs:

```
// Program: Press to Light Up
// -------------------------------------------------------

#include "SparkButton/SparkButton.h"
SparkButton button = SparkButton();
void setup(){
  button.begin();
}
void loop(){

  // Check if Button 1 - denoted by the "1" in parentheses of the
  // buttonOn function - is pressed, and if true, make all LEDs
  // glow red for 2 sec
  if (button.buttonOn(1)) {
    // Make all LEDs glow red for 2 seconds
    button.allLedsOn(255, 0, 0);
    delay(2000);
    button.allLedsOff();
  }
  // Check if all 4 buttons are pressed
  if (button.allButtonsOn()) {
    // Make LED 6 glow blue for 2 seconds. The format here
    // ledOn(LED, red, green, blue), where LED is the LED-number
    // and red, green, blue are the brightness values as usual.
```

```
      button.ledOn(6, 0, 0, 255);
      delay(2000);
      button.allLedsOff();
    }
}
```

This completes our second program. You should be able to flash it to your device from the Web IDE, and test the program by pressing Button 1 or all the buttons together!

Tweets and e-mail

We have explored two functionalities using the Internet Button in the previous sections. As part of our next functionality, we will send a tweet from our device when the Internet Button is shaken. The tweet is sent using the **Arduino Tweet Library** (http://arduino-twe et.appspot.com/). This library is used as a proxy between the Particle board and Twitter, and it makes it easy to post tweets, as it takes care of authentication using OAuth.

We will also send an e-mail when Button 1 is pressed. When Button 2 is pressed, we will fetch a tweet, and display it in the serial console.

The code for this program is broken into five parts since it is long. Also, we will omit comments for lines that have been explained previously.

In the Web IDE, create a new application. Type in or copy the following code into the Web IDE's editor:

```
// Program: Shake to tweet, press to email
// -----------------------------------------------------

#include "SparkButton/SparkButton.h"
#include "math.h"

// Generate the OAuth Token from the Arduino Tweet Library
// website and replace "XXXXX" below, with the Token
#define TOKEN "XXXXX"

// Twitter Proxy Service by Arduino Tweet Library
#define LIB_DOMAIN "arduino-tweet.appspot.com"

// Declare a variable for the TCP Client which is used
// for sending an HTTP Request
TCPClient client;
SparkButton button = SparkButton();
int currX, currY, currZ;
int prevX, prevY, prevZ;
```

```
// Variables to store time threshold for sending tweet
// and motion threshold to trigger the tweet-sending event
int time_thold, motion_thold;
```

Thus far, we've declared some variables we'll be needing for this program. We also created an instance of the SparkButton, which we will be using to manage the Internet Button. Continuing with the code, add the following:

```
// This is the TwitterFetch webhook's callback function. It gets
// called when the Twitter Service URL returns data.
// Here, we're making LED 8 glow Blue for 2 seconds whenever
// Twitter data (tweet) is received
void twitterHandler(const char *name, const char *data) {
  button.ledOn(8, 0, 0, 255);

  // Print the incoming data to the serial console
  // for debugging purposes
  Serial.println("-----------Twitter Handler---------------");
  Serial.print("NAME - ");
  Serial.println(name);
  Serial.print("DATA - ");
  Serial.println(data);
  Serial.println();
  Serial.println("-------------------End-------------------");

  delay(2000);
  button.allLedsOff();
}

// This is the email callback function. This function is called
// after an email is sent successfully. Here, we're making LED 10
// glow Green for 2 seconds when this happens.
void mailHandler(const char *name, const char *data) {

  button.ledOn(10, 0, 255, 0);
  Serial.println("-----------Email Handler---------------");
  Serial.println("Email has been sent successfully!");
  Serial.println("-------------------End-------------------");
  delay(2000);
  button.allLedsOff();
}
```

In the second part of our program, we defined two functions known as callbacks. These callback functions get called whenever the event associated with them is triggered, as described in the comments within the code.

The following is the third part of this program, where we define a function to post a message to Twitter using the Arduino Tweet Library:

```
// Method to post tweet to Twitter
void post(){
  // Create the message to post to Twitter
  Message = "Accelerometer readings:";
  Message += "(" + currX + ", " + currY + ", " + currZ + ")";

  // Save message string as a Character Array into "msg"
  Message.toCharArray(msg, 128);
  // Connect to the Arduino Tweet Library and, if we are indeed
  // connected, print a message to the Serial Console.
  if (client.connect(LIB_DOMAIN, 80)) {
    Serial.println("Connected to Twitter Library");
  }
  if (client.connected()) {
    // Send (post) the message as the Twitter Status
    // along with the authentication Token
    client.println("POST /update HTTP/1.0");
    client.println("Host: " + LIB_DOMAIN);
    client.print("Content-Length: ");
    client.println(strlen(msg) + strlen(TOKEN) + 14);
    client.println(("token=" + TOKEN);
    client.print("&status=" + msg);
  }
  else
  {
    Serial.println();
    Serial.println("Could not connect. Try again.");
  }
  client.stop();
}
```

The next part of the program defines the one-time setup function:

```
void setup() {
  button.begin();

  //Start the Serial Communication Port with a speed of 9600 baud
  Serial.begin(9600);
  // Make LED 2 glow green with about half brightness
  button.ledOn(2, 0, 100, 0);

  // Wait for the Serial Communication to be established
  while (!Serial.available()){
    SPARK_WLAN_Loop();
  }
```

```
// Subscribe to the webhook response event and specify the
// callback function for receiving the response from the
// Twitter fetch URL invokation. The format of the webhook
// response event name is 'hook-response/<webhook-event-name>'
bool subscribed = Spark.subscribe("hook-response/twitterFetch",
twitterHandler, MY_DEVICES);

if (subscribed){
  // Make LED 3 glow Green for 2 sec with about half
  // brightness to notify the subscription was successful
  button.ledOn(3, 0, 100, 0);
  delay(2000);
  button.allLedsOff();
} else {

  // Make LED 3 glow Red for 2 sec with about half
  // brightness to notify the subscription failed
  button.ledOn(3, 100, 0, 0);
  delay(2000);
  button.allLedsOff();
}
// Subscribe to the mailgun webhook response event and specify
// the callback function for receiving the response from the
// Mailgun service.
subscribed = Spark.subscribe("hook-response/mailgun",
mailHandler, MY_DEVICES);
if (subscribed){
  // Make LED 6 glow Green at half brightness
  // to notify the subscription was successful
  button.ledOn(6, 0, 100, 0);
  delay(2000);
  button.allLedsOff();
} else {

  // Make LED 6 glow Red at half brightness
  // to notify the subscription failed
  button.ledOn(6, 100, 0, 0);
  delay(2000);
  button.allLedsOff();
}
 // Notify on the serial monitor that setup has run
// successfully and the Loop is about to begin
Serial.println("Setup Completed");

// Read accelerometer values as previous values
prevX = button.readX();
prevY = button.readY();
prevZ = button.readZ();
```

```
// Set the motion threshold to 50 (arrived
// at by trial and error) and time threshold to 0
motion_thold = 50;
time_thold = 0;
}
```

The next part of the code defines the loop that iterates indefinitely, checking for the motion threshold and time threshold, and performing some actions accordingly:

```
void loop() {

// Read the current values of the accelerometer
currX = button.readX();
currY = button.readY();
currZ = button.readZ();

// Check if motion beyond the threshold is detected, i.e.,
// the Internet Button was shaken
if(abs (currX - prevX) > motion_thold ||
abs (currY - prevY) > motion_thold ||
abs (currZ - prevZ) > motion_thold) {

// Post a message with the accelerometer values to Twitter
post();

// Make LEDs 7,6,5 glow Red, Green, and Blue for 1 second
button.ledOn(7, 100, 0, 0);
button.ledOn(6, 0, 100, 0);
button.ledOn(5, 0, 0, 100);
delay(1000);
button.allLedsOff();
}

// If button 1 is pressed, make all LEDs glow green for 1
second
// and trigger the mailgun event to send an email using mailgun
if(button.buttonOn(1)){
Serial.println("button 1 is pressed");
button.allLedsOn(0, 255, 0);
delay(1000);
Spark.publish("mailgun","");
button.allLedsOff();
}

// If button 2 is pressed, make all LEDs glow red for 1 second
// and trigger the twitterFetch event to get a tweet using
// the Twitter webhook. The tweet will be printed in the serial
// console
```

```
if(button.buttonOn(2)){
Serial.println("button 2 is pressed");
button.allLedsOn(255, 0, 0);
delay(1000);
Spark.publish("twitterFetch","");
button.allLedsOff();
}

// set current accelerometer values to previous values and
// prepare for the next loop iteration
prevX = currX;
prevY = currY;
prevZ = currZ;

// Decrement the time threshold at the end of this iteration
time_thold--;

// Slow down each iteration to one per second
delay(1000);
}
```

This completes the code for the Twitter and e-mail interaction project, and we have implemented all the functionalities that we set out to build.

You should now be familiar with working with Particle Photon and Core.

Troubleshooting

When running some of our code on Particle boards, more so in the Core, it might occasionally not work as expected. Some of the problems you might face are listed here:

- **Particle CLI setup and other commands fail**: This is usually due to Internet connectivity issues. Make sure your Wi-Fi is turned on, and the computer is connected to Wi-Fi.
- **Web requests fail to work**: This problem arises due to the low memory available in Particle boards running old firmware, particularly the Core. The available memory is sometimes not enough for web responses to fit into. This problem can be rectified by updating the Core to the latest firmware, and slowing down the frequency of web requests. Flashing the latest firmware is discussed in *Chapter 6, Hacking the Firmware*.

- Flashing new code takes a lot of time, in the order of minutes, while normally it should be less than 30 seconds. Sometimes, old code still remains after flashing—this problem is fairly common in the Particle Core. It may be due to a weak Wi-Fi network. The problem can be fixed by flashing the firmware using USB instead of Wi-Fi. Flashing the Core is generally slower compared to flashing the Photon due to the fact that the firmware and application code are both being sent simultaneously to the Core. The problem is fixed in the Photon by sending only the application code on deployment rather than sending both together.

Summary

In this chapter, we had a high-level, 360-degree view into the world of the Particle Photon, its Internet Button accessory, and its software. We saw how we can program the Photon to interact with the external world. In the chapters that follow, we will take you into the internals of each component of the Particle IoT ecosystem, and you will be able to use the Particle boards to their full potential. Particle has created an excellent end-to-end ecosystem to make IoT application building very quick and simple. The open source firmware, integration with the cloud, excellent documentation, technical support, and the huge user base on active forums let a user easily develop a good understanding of IoT boards and the IoT ecosystem in a very short time.

3
P2P and Local Server

In this chapter, you will be introduced to the two following popular network architectures for data transmission or communication between devices:

1. Client-server
2. Peer-to-peer (P2P)

You will also learn how to use these architectures in the Particle ecosystem.

We will develop a P2P application using **Cylon.js** (`https://cylonjs.com/`), a Javascript framework for robotics, physical computing, and IoT, to control our Particle device and an onboard LED with the keyboard. We will then describe how to set up the Particle server on your local machine for fast transmission of data across various devices, and we will end the chapter with a brief introduction to other protocols used in the IoT sphere.

The topics covered in this chapter are as follows:

- Client-server versus P2P networks
- Setting up a P2P network for Particle devices
- Local server setup
- Alternate protocols for IoT

Client-server versus P2P networks ÂÂ

This section starts by describing the traditional client-server architecture, and goes on to describe how the P2P architecture works. The section ends with a comparison between P2P and client-server architectures.

Traditional client-server architecture

Client-server architecture is a network architecture in which each node (computer or device) on the network is either a client or a server. It is based on the consumer model, that is, the clients consume what is available on the servers. Servers are powerful computers dedicated to managing network traffic and other shared resources such as disk drives and printers. Servers provide services via various protocols like **Hyper Text Transfer Protocol (HTTP)** and **Hyper Text Transfer Protocol Secure (HTTPS)**.

Clients are the nodes on the network that consume services provided by the servers. The client nodes need not be as powerful as servers. What makes the difference in computing power requirement is that a few servers-sometimes, just one-usually have to service many clients, and hence the server has to process a lot more data than the clients. Simplistically, servers have to run many processing threads simultaneously, whereas clients need to run only one processing thread.

Clients and servers exchange messages in a request-response manner. The client initiates communication by generating a **request,** and sends it to server using one of the client-server protocols such as HTTP or HTTPS. Once a server receives a request from any client, it creates a process or thread for the client, and the server goes about processing the request using the process or thread created. Upon completion of processing the request, the server sends a **response** to the client, and optionally, closes the connection.

Peer-to-peer network architecture

P2P architecture works with direct communication between nodes without any authority managing or handling the connections. Here, there is no need for a central server or entity. The nodes that communicate in the P2P network are called **peers**. Peers share resources with each other, such as processing power, disk storage, and network bandwidth. P2P networks are designed around the notion of equal peer nodes simultaneously functioning as both clients and servers for the other nodes on the network.

P2P networks are scalable, and with an increase in the number of nodes in a network, the performance tends to increase (up to a point). The explanation for the increase in performance is that with an increase in the number of nodes, the number of nodes providing a service (in server mode) increases, hence increasing the availability; the total server workload per node decreases, leading to a better overall performance.

P2P networks have been successfully used for powering file-sharing applications over the Internet, for example, **BitTorrent**. In this chapter, we explore the use of P2P for communication among Particle boards without having to go through the Internet.

Client-server versus P2P

The following table compares features of the client-server and P2P architectures:

Client-server	P2P
Multiple client computers connect to a single server computer or a few server computers for availing services and information.	A group of peer computers connect together for sharing of resources and information.
The performance is dependent on how powerful the server(s) is/are. There is performance degradation when the number of client computers connected to a given server increases.	The performance of the network becomes better when more peer computers or nodes join the network.
There is no sharing of resources among the connected clients, and the resource sharing workload is handled by a single (or few) server(s).	The resource sharing workload is shared among all the connected peers.
In case of server node failure, the service is not available, and all the clients lose connectivity until the server is online. (In case of a client node failure, other clients continue to get service.)	In case of one or more node failures, there is no significant loss of service to any of the active peers.

Advantages and disadvantages of P2P networking

Each technology has its pros and cons in a given situation. In this section, we present the advantages and disadvantages of using P2P networks with IoT devices.

The advantages of a P2P network are as follows:

- A P2P network setup is simple as compared to setting up a server for a client-server network
- A P2P network is very cost effective
- It is easy to share files and resources within the P2P network
- It is very efficient when the number of nodes is large

The disadvantages of a P2P network are as follows:

- In P2P, no security is provided out of the box, and access levels have to be defined and implemented by ourselves
- In P2P, it is difficult to track the source of information
- In a P2P file-sharing scenario, often multiple versions of the same file are available, causing ambiguity

Setting up a P2P network for Particle devices

Out of the box, Particle boards run the stock firmware which integrates with the Particle cloud; thus, Particle devices are in the client-server mode when you buy them. It is not possible to set up a P2P network with the stock firmware shipped with Particle boards, and hence we need to flash a custom firmware onto the device, that supports the P2P protocol. **VoodooSpark** (`https://github.com/voodootikigod/voodoospark`) is a customized firmware build for Particle devices, which allows remote access of the firmware API using a TCP connection.

Flash the VoodooSpark firmware

The VoodooSpark firmware can be deployed very easily using the Web IDE at Particle Build (`https://build.particle.io`). Copy and paste the code available at `https://raw.githubusercontent.com/voodootikigod/voodoospark/master/firmware/voodoospark.cpp` in your Web IDE editor window, and click the Flash button (⚡). This will burn the custom firmware onto your Particle Photon.

Connect the Particle board with VoodooSpark

To use VoodooSpark firmware on your Particle device, you will need the **DEVICE-ID** of the Particle board you're using, and the Particle Build **ACCESS-TOKEN**, which you can obtain from the Settings tab (⚙) in the Web IDE at `https://build.particle.io`. You will need to send a GET request to the Particle cloud using a web browser or a command-line tool like **cURL**. The URL to send the request to is `https://api.particle.io/v1/devices/{DEVICE-ID}/endpoint?access_token={ACCESS-TOKEN}`.

Sending this request will return a response of the following form:

```
{
  "cmd": "VarReturn",
  "name": "endpoint",
  "result": "192.168.1.10:48879",
  "coreInfo": {
    "last_app": "",
    "last_heard": "2014-05-08T02:51:48.826Z",
    "connected": true,
    "deviceID": "{DEVICE-ID}"
  }
}
```

In the response data, the `"result"` attribute gives the local IP address and port of the Particle device. VoodooSpark communicates with the Particle board using TCP connections to this IP address and port.

Controlling your Particle board using the keyboard

In this section of the chapter, we will build an application, that controls the LED present on the Particle device using the computer's keyboard. VoodooSpark provides a way to program the Particle device using Node.js (https://Node.js.org/), a Javascript runtime that allows programming using the Javascript language. This means it helps us leverage the Node.js package ecosystem, npm, which is the largest ecosystem of open source libraries in the world. The npm (https://www.npmjs.org) package management tool, bundled with the Node.js installation, is used to download and install Node.js libraries or packages.

If you haven't installed Node.js already, you should install it now using instructions at the Node.js website. Once Node.js is installed, you can check if it is installed correctly with the following command:

```
$ node -v
V4.4.7
```

If you do not see the version number in the output, you may have to add the Node.js bin directory to the PATH environment variable.

We will begin by creating a directory for the project called `particle-keyboard` by running the following commands from the command line of our computer:

```
$ mkdir particle-keyboard
```

Next, let's go ahead and install the required Cylon.js libraries in the directory created in the preceding step:

```
$ cd particle-keyboard
$ npm install cylon cylon-spark cylon-keyboard
```

Now we'll write some Node.js code for controlling the LED on the Particle device. The LED can be turned ON by setting the **D7** pin as HIGH. Our code will be written such that on pressing the Up key on the computer's keyboard, the LED on the board will glow, and on pressing the Down button, the LED will turn off.

Create a new text file called up-down-led.js using a text editor in the particle-keyboard directory that we created earlier. Copy the following code into the new up-down-led.js file, and save it:

```
// Program: Use Up/Down arrow Keys to Control LED
// ----------------------------------------------

// Use the Cylon.js library
var Cylon = require('cylon');

// Setup or initialize the Cylon object with the
// connection details, device details and work function
Cylon.robot(

  // JSON object containing initialization details begins here
  {

    connections: {
               keyboard: {adaptor: 'keyboard'},
               spark: {
                 adaptor: 'spark',
                 accessToken: 'YOUR_ACCESS_TOKEN',
                 deviceId: 'YOUR_DEVICE_ID'
               }
             },

    devices: {
      led: {driver: 'led', pin:'D7'},
      keyboard: {driver: 'keyboard'}
    },

    work: function(my) {
      console.log('CONNECTED - PRESS UP OR DOWN KEY TO CONTROL
      LED');

      my.keyboard.on('UP', function(key){
```

```
      my.led.turnOn();
    });
    my.keyboard.on('DOWN', function(key){
      my.led.turnOff();
    });
  }
  // JSON object containing initialization details ends here
  }
);
```

Replace `'YOUR_ACCESS_TOKEN'` and `'YOUR_DEVICE_ID'` with actual values, and save the `up-down-led.js` file. Make sure that both the computer and the Particle device are on the same network. This is necessary for the connections to work. Now let's go ahead and run the program from the command line, as follows:

```
$ node up-down-led.js
```

Once the program starts, you should see the following message displayed on the terminal:

CONNECTED – PRESS UP OR DOWN KEY TO CONTROL LED

Now, pressing the Up key on the keyboard should light up the blue LED on the Particle device, and pressing the Down key should turn it off.

We have successfully controlled an LED with a keyboard!

Local server setup

As we have seen earlier, Particle provides a cloud-based development environment for building and deploying code to its devices. The Particle cloud is also the gateway through which all communication to and from the Particle device happens. This works well if you have a good Internet connection, however, it may become slow and unreliable if you have a slow connection. This becomes a problem in certain situations where you need to access the board, for example, to read values from it in real time. Your application may require real-time performance, which the cloud-based setup may not be able to guarantee.

By using the Particle cloud, data from your board located in your living room is sent to the server on the Internet, and data comes back from the Internet server to your home router that is also in the same living room. All the traffic over the relatively slow Internet adds latency to the data flow, even when the devices are in the same local network.

The problem just discussed can be overcome by setting up the Particle server on one of your local computers at home or work. Particle has open sourced their server code. It is available at `https://github.com/spark/spark-server`. In a later section of this chapter, we will see how to set up a local Particle server. The local server does not compile user programs yet, and we will still need to use the cloud-based Particle build tool at `https://build.particl e.io` to compile our program and get the firmware. `Chapter 6`, *Hacking the Firmware* covers how to compile programs remotely, and deploy the firmware to the devices using USB.

Advantages and disadvantages of Particle local server

The following are the advantages of a Particle local server:

- The network latency is reduced, leading to almost real-time data transfer
- Any data security and privacy concerns are addressed, as data is stored and passed around in the local network, and it does not leave the local network

The disadvantages of a Particle local server are as follows:

- The local server does not include Particle Build functions
- The setup is an additional task, and with it comes an added cost of maintenance
- The local server software needs to be updated regularly to get new features and bug fixes

Installing Particle server on a local machine

The Particle server code can be downloaded from the following link:

`https://github.com/spark/spark-server/archive/master.zip`

The server code is a Node.js package. It has dependencies on other Node.js modules. These dependencies are automatically downloaded when installing the server application.

Unzip the file, and navigate to the root directory of the project with the following commands:

```
$ unzip master.zip
$ cd spark-server-master
```

After making sure you have Node.js with npm installed as well as Internet connectivity, from the command line run the `npm install` command as follows:

```
$ npm install
```

The install command fetches all the required dependencies from the npm repository on the Internet, and installs them in a `node_modules` subfolder at the root of the project.

Configuring the local server

By now you should have installed the Particle server on one of your local machines. Now it's time to run the server, and configure the Particle board to point to your local server installation.

To run your server, navigate to the root directory of the Spark server (we'll assume you've already done that), and run the following command on your command line:

```
$ node main.js
```

The preceding command fires up your local server, and, among other things, prints the IP address and port to which your Particle board must connect. The information is printed on the terminal as follows:

```
$ node main.js
. . .
. . .
Starting server, listening on <your_port>
. . .
. . .
Your server IP address is: <your_ip_address>
. . .
```

It's time to configure the local server credentials and the public key in the Particle board. First we need to put the Particle Core or Photon in the **Device Firmware Upgrade (DFU)** mode by following the steps given next:

1. Hold down both the RESET and MODE buttons of the device.

2. Release only the RESET button while continuing to hold down the MODE button.

3. Wait for the LED to start flashing yellow.

4. Release the MODE button.

While in the DFU mode, you can access the firmware or flash new firmware onto the device manually. This mode will be covered in detail in *Burning firmware using Particle-CLI*, in `Chapter 6`, *Hacking the Firmware*.

When the server starts for the first time, it creates the server public key and private key-pair files in the root directory of the server application. These files are named `default_key.pub.pem` (public key) and `default_key.pem` (private key). We will use the public key file in the next step.

The Particle command-line client is used to load your server's public key and IP address onto your Photon or Core. The command to do this is as follows:

```
$ particle keys server default_key.pub.pem <your_ip_address>
```

Once the server's public key and IP address load are successful, the command also converts the `pem` file into a `der` file.

Next you have to change the Particle-CLI configuration to point to the local server instead of Particle cloud. You can do this by updating the JSON configuration file generated by particle-CLI. Using your favorite text editor, open up the configuration file at `<Your-Home-Directory>/.particle/particle.config.json`, and add the following snippet to the JSON file (after adding a comma at the end of the existing content in the file), save, and close it:

```
{
    "apiUrl": "http://<your_ip_address>"
}
```

Now we have to put the Particle device in listening mode by pressing the MODE button until the **blue** LED flashes. Once this happens, run the following command from the command line to get the device ID:

```
$ particle identify
Your device id is 390xxxxxxxxxxxxxxxxxxx031
```

The preceding command will print the *core_id* or *photon_id* of your device on the terminal. Note down this ID. Next we have to create a user, and log in using the Particle-CLI.

Run the following command to do so:

```
$ particle setup
```

This last command starts a wizard as explained in *Connecting Particle Photon or Core*, in Chapter 2, *Fire Up Your Kit* . Follow the wizard to create a user (if you haven't done so already), and log in using the same wizard.

Once logged in, you have to provision the access to the local server using the Particle-CLI by running the following command at the command line:

```
$ particle keys doctor <photon/core_id>
```

Now your local server should have registered the Core or Photon, and this can be verified by running the following command from your command line:

```
$ particle list
Checking with the cloud...
Retrieving devices... (this might take a few seconds)
my_device_name (0123456789ABCDEFGHI) 0 variables, and 4
functions
Functions:
  int digitalWrite(string)
  int digitalRead(string)
  int analogWrite(string)
  int analogRead(string)
```

This completes the setup of a local server on your own machine. You have also bound your Particle board to your local server. The functions that are currently supported by the local server can be found at https://github.com/spark/spark-server.

Alternate protocols for IoT

IoT devices are constrained in terms of computing and memory resources, and Particle devices are no exception. The REST architecture has been used extensively on the web for communication between clients and servers. Using the same architecture for IoT or resource-constrained devices is not very optimal. It leads to packet losses or memory being full, which result in unwanted behavior. The REST implementation is also process intensive for the IoT devices, thereby putting a heavy load on these tiny devices.

To overcome these issues, new protocols and architecture have been designed. We will be presenting briefly some of these new protocols, which are better suited for IoT.

MQTT

The first protocol we look at is called **MQ Telemetry Transport(MQTT)** (http://www.mqtt.org). Historically, the "MQ" in MQTT came from IBM's MQ Series message queuing (https://en.wikipedia.org/wiki/Message_queuing) product line.

MQTT is a publish-subscribe-based (https://en.wikipedia.org/wiki/Publish%E2%8%93subscribe_pattern) lightweight messaging protocol for use on top of the TCP/IP protocol (https://en.wikipedia.org/wiki/TCP/IP). It is designed for connections with remote locations where a small code footprint is required or the network bandwidth is limited.

MQTT is widely used in a range of home automation and small devices, and is gaining popularity with healthcare providers to provide real-time data to doctors using various sensors.

Andy Stanford-Clark (https://en.wikipedia.org/wiki/Andy_Stanford-Clark) and Arlen Nipper of Cirrus Link Solutions (http://www.cirrus-link.com/) authored the first version of the protocol in 1999. In 2013, IBM submitted MQTT v3.1 to the OASIS (https://en.wikipedia.org/wiki/OASIS_(organization) and https://www.oasis-open.org/) specification body, opening up the specification, but limiting any further major changes. MQTT is now an ISO standard (ISO/IEC PRF 20922).

MQTT supports username and password authentication. In order to make the protocol more secure, it can be encrypted using SSL, but SSL adds significant network overhead. Cylon.js has support for MQTT out of the box, and can be used with Particle devices using the Cylon-MQTT module. More information on MQTT can be found at http://www.mqtt.org.

CoAP

The second protocol we look at is a distant cousin of REST, called **Constrained Application Protocol (CoAP)** (http://coap.technology/). CoAP is a specialized web transfer protocol for use with IoT devices, and is based on the widely successful REST model. In this protocol, servers make resources available under a URL, and clients access these resources using methods such as GET, PUT, POST, and DELETE.

CoAP has been designed to work on microcontrollers with as low as 10 KB of RAM and 100 KB of code space. It is very developer-friendly, and does not feel different than HTTP, which has been used widely for web programming. CoAP was developed as an Internet Standards document, RFC 7252 (http://coap.technology/spec.html).

CoAP is secure and uses **Datagram Transport Layer Security (DTLS)**, which is as good as 3072-bit RSA keys and is resource friendly. It supports different types of payloads, and integrates easily with XML, JSON, and **Concise Binary Object Representation (CBOR)**. One of the compelling features of CoAP is device discovery, wherein it provides a way to discover the properties of the nodes on the network, which is very helpful in M2M communication. More information on CoAP can be found at http://coap.technology.

In addition to these, some more IoT protocols and links for further reading material are given in the following table:

Protocol	Details
MQTT	**Home**: http://mqtt.org/ **Wikipedia**: https://en.wikipedia.org/wiki/MQTT
CoAP	**Home**: http://coap.technology/ **Wikipedia**: https://en.wikipedia.org/wiki/Constrained_Application_Protocol
Advanced Message Queuing Protocol (AMQP)	**Home**: https://www.amqp.org/ **Wikipedia**: https://en.wikipedia.org/wiki/Advanced_Message_Queuing_Protocol
WebSocket	**Wikipedia**: https://en.wikipedia.org/wiki/WebSocket
Extensible Messaging and Presence Protocol (XMPP)	**Home**: https://xmpp.org/ **Wikipedia**: https://en.wikipedia.org/wiki/XMPP

Summary

In this chapter, our aim was to give you a feel of the internal workings of the networks and communication protocols using which Particle devices are deployed. New ways to connect various Particle devices and enable integration between them have been presented. We also described how to set up a P2P network using the VoodooSpark firmware and Cylon.js module, which will be used extensively for the projects in the upcoming chapters. We presented you with instructions to deploy a local server instance of Particle cloud, which can be used for near real-time communication between various devices by removing the need for moving the data to the Internet and back. Finally, we ended the chapter with an introduction to other popular protocols and architectures which are in place for IoT devices and deserve looking into.

4

Connecting the Sensors

In this chapter, you will learn to build a smart kitchen using a network of Photons. A smart kitchen consists of a smart inventory management system which is linked to a cloud-based data store.

An RFID reader connected to a Photon scans each product brought to the kitchen. A motion sensor connected to another Photon monitors the movement of the kitchen cabinet doors to keep track of the location and usage of each grocery item inside the kitchen. The Photon connected to the motion sensor sends the item location to the other Photon connected to the RFID reader, which, in turn, relays the consolidated information to the cloud store. Periodic and event-triggered data analysis of the cloud storage data sends SMS notifications to the user about the inventory status like product expiry, unused products, inefficient storage, and so on.

The topics covered in this chapter are as follows:

- Overview of the project
- Hardware components and setup
- Communication between two Photons
- Data storage on the cloud
- Cloud data analysis and SMS notification
- Troubleshooting

Overview of the project

We will set up the project in a medium-sized kitchen with a single entry. We monitor the items brought into the kitchen using Photons. Items that are brought into the kitchen are stored across three cabinets. The user has to follow a strict routine in order for us to keep the implementation aligned to the scope of this chapter. We assume that all grocery items have an RFID tag. After grocery shopping is done, the first thing to do is to scan each of the items using the RFID reader attached to the Photon placed near the kitchen entrance. After the entry of the item is recorded, the item is stored in one of the three cabinets. Thus, scanning and storing is a strictly ordered action pair. Similarly, when taking out an item from the cabinet, it needs to be scanned by the RFID reader as soon as it is out of the cabinet. The motion sensor connected to the doors of the cabinet monitors the inventory movement or usage. The Photon with the RFID reader, near the kitchen entrance, acts as a gateway to the cloud storage where all the inventory data-storage and data-analysis happens. *Figure 1* illustrates the project flow:

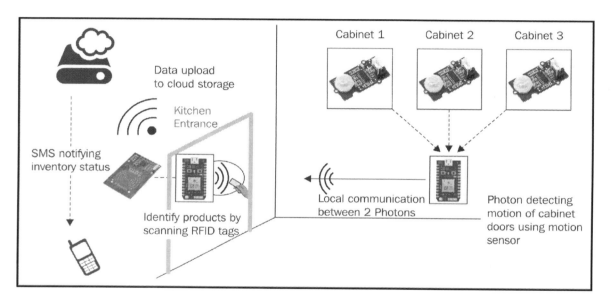

Figure 1: Overview of smart kitchen inventory management system

Hardware components and setup

The following is a list of the hardware components and the quantity of each needed to build the smart kitchen project:

- Photons (2)
- Li-Po batteries (2)
- 3-6V DC power supply (2)

- RFID Reader module RFID-RC522 (1)
- RFID tags (6)
- Passive infrared (PIR) motion sensors (3)
- Jumper wires (20)
- Breadboards (2)

We will describe some of these components in detail, and explain the function they perform.

RFID reader module RC522-RFID and RFID tags

Radio frequency identification (RFID) is a **Near Field Communication (NFC)** technology, where two devices can transfer data between them using radio waves when they are near each other:

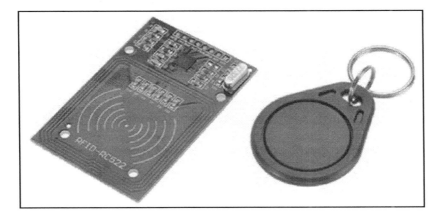

Figure 2: MIFARE RC522 RFID reader module (left) and RFID tag (right)

We use the RC522-RFID module from MIFARE (https://www.mifare.net/).

The RFID module needs to be powered by a 3.3V DC power source. It reads the tag ID numbers of the RFID tags near it, and passes them to the Photon to which it is connected. The tags are passive, and don't need any power supply. In *Figure 2*, the board on the left is the RFID reader module and an RFID tag (key fob) is on the right. RFID tags are available in other forms too, like stickers, cards, and so on. Each tag has a unique ID. The ID is read over an encrypted channel to ensure data security.

The RFID reader communicates with the Photon it is connected to over a **Serial Peripheral Interface (SPI)** (https://en.wikipedia.org/wiki/Serial_Peripheral_Interface_Bus). *Figure 3* illustrates the connection and communication between the Reader and the Photon. Microcontrollers like Photon (master) use synchronous serial data protocol for high-speed communication with peripheral devices like the RFID reader (slave) over short distances. We will use the analog pins of the Photon to connect with the RFID module:

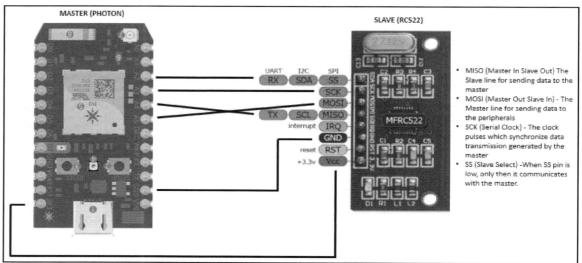

Figure 3: Connection diagram for Photon to RFID reader

PIR motion sensor

There are many PIR (https://en.wikipedia.org/wiki/Passive_infrared_sensor) motion sensors out there in the market. We decided to work with the Grove sensor from Seeed Studio (http://www.seeedstudio.com/), as it is very simple to work with. Seeed Studio provides extensive guides and tutorials along with libraries to use its sensors. The Grove kit includes a Base Shield, which makes the connection to the master easy as well. In our project, we will use jumper wires to connect the motion sensor to the Photon. The following image shows the Grove PIR sensor:

Figure 4: Grove PIR motion sensor

Most objects emit heat, which is **electromagnetic (EM)** radiation in the infrared part of the EM spectrum. This radiated light is invisible to the human eye, but PIR sensors can detect light in this normally invisible wavelength.

A PIR sensor works by changing the output voltage at its signal or SIG pin whenever it senses a change in the IR radiation within its field of view. The following diagram shows the connections between the Photon and the PIR sensor:

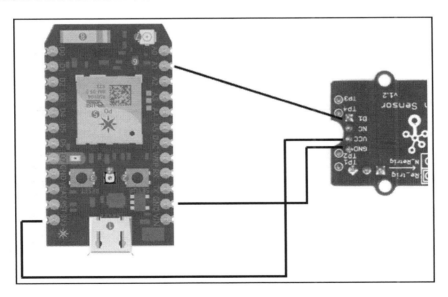

Figure 5: Connection diagram for Photon to PIR motion sensor

As seen in the preceding connection diagram, we have connected the motion sensor's SIG pin to an analog pin of the Photon. This gives us a value in a range. However, it can be connected to any digital pin as well. A digital pin gives a 0 or 1 for absence or presence of motion. For detecting motion, the number read from the pin doesn't matter to us as long as we can detect the change in the number.

Data flow diagrams

Now that you know what each of the hardware components do, it's time to put everything together and see them come to life!

The data flow and sequence of events when an item is stored in the kitchen cabinet is shown in the following diagram:

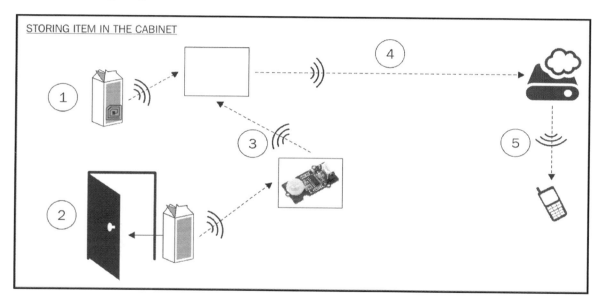

Figure 6: Data flow and sequence when storing items in kitchen

In the preceding diagram, the numbered circles show the sequence of events, and the dotted arrows show the data flow.

Before storing an item inside a cabinet, the item is scanned at the kitchen's entrance using the RFID reader connected to a Photon (**1**). This Photon waits till it receives a cabinet location from the other Photon. The PIR motion sensor connected to the other Photon detects movement of the particular cabinet the item was stored in, and sends its cabinet address (**2**) to the motion sensor Photon. The motion-sensor-Photon sends the cabinet address to the first Photon (**3**). Once the item's location is received, the first Photon sends the latest inventory update to the cloud storage (**4**). To keep it simple, we assume that the actions of the RFID tag scanning and putting the item into the cabinet will occur in sequence, consistently.

Based on the latest data, the user is informed via an SMS (**5**) if anything related to the new item needs their attention (for example, "New item kept in the wrong cupboard", "There are already similar items present in the kitchen and the user should use them first before unpacking the new item", and so on). Instead of sending an SMS, you can send push notifications to the phone as well.

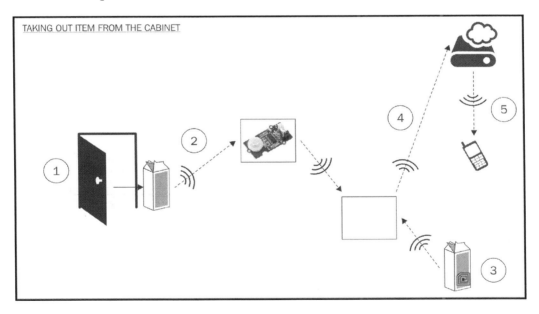

Figure 7: Data flow and sequence when taking out items from cabinet

In the preceding diagram, the numbered circles show the sequence of events, and the dotted arrows show the data flow.

When an item is taken out of the cabinet, the motion sensor registers motion (**1**), and sends the cabinet address to the Photon it is connected to (**2**). Now, the item is scanned using the RFID reader. The reader sends the item's ID to the second Photon to which the RFID reader is connected (**3**). Once the item's ID is received, the second Photon sends the latest inventory update to the cloud storage (**4**). As soon as the inventory status is updated, an SMS alert is sent to the user for the item taken out of the cabinet. ("There is already an older item in the cabinet", and the like.)

Communication between the Photons

In the projects described so far in this book, we have been dealing with only one Photon device, which acted as the central processing unit for the project. In the real world, we often come up with solutions that require multiple processing devices.

In this section, we will build a small prototype which will help you send data from one Photon to another. The code for this project will be written in the online Web IDE provided by the Particle hosted at `https://build.particle.io`. We will use the `Particle.publish`method to publish events to the Particle cloud. Any device which has subscribed to this event by using the `Particle.subscribe` method gets a notification, and the corresponding event handler function is executed. The name of the event can be set from the code, and additional data can be passed from the publisher device to the subscriber device as part of the event message.

In this example, we will create a system consisting of two Photon devices which are connected to the Particle Cloud. Let's say our Photon devices are named P1 and P2; P1 is connected to a motion sensor, and P2 is connected to an LED. Whenever motion is detected at P1, it sends out an event which is received by P2. Upon receiving the message, P2 toggles the state of the LED connected to it.

Connect the motion sensor to the Photon P1 as described in *Figure 5*. On the Photon P2, connect the LED on pin D7, making sure that the longer leg of the LED (anode) is connected to D7, and the shorter leg of the LED (cathode) is connected to the **ground** (**GND**) terminal.

Sample code

Fire up your Particle Build in the web browser and create a new app, giving it any name you want. Now write the following code for Photon P1 in the editing area:

```
// Set the powerPin variable to the D7 digital I/O pin
int powerPin = D7;

// Set the motionSensorPin to the A0 analog I/O pin
int motionSensorPin = A0;

// Declare a variable for holding the motion sensor value
int sensorValue;
```

We use the LED on P1 to indicate the power supply, and pin A0 takes in the input from the motion sensor. The `sensorValue` variable is used to store the motion sensor data.

We set up the board by configuring the mode of each pin we're going to use. Pin D7 (the power indicator) should be set to output mode, and pin A0 (the motion sensor) should be set to input mode. To do this, add the following code to the `setup()` function:

```
void setup() {

  // Sets the D7 pin as an output pin
  pinMode ( powerPin, OUTPUT );
  // Set the A0 pin as an input pin
  pinMode ( motionSensorPin, INPUT );
}
```

The `loop()` function gets called indefinitely, so this is where we keep checking for motion and take appropriate action. We do this by repeatedly reading the sensor value on the `motionSensorPin` (A0) pin, and checking if the value is above a threshold. A threshold value of `4000` seems to work well. When the sensor value read is above this threshold, we send a message that says `"on"`, and when the value is below the threshold, we send an `"off"` message. This is done in the `loop()` function, as follows:

```
void loop() {

  // Read the motion sensor value
  sensorValue = analogRead(motionSensorPin);
  // Compare the sensor value with the threshold (4000)
  if (sensorValue > 4000) {

    Particle.publish("motion_alert", "on");  // Send "on"
```

```
  } else {
    Particle.publish("motion_alert", "off"); // Send "off"
  }
}
```

We send the on/off message using the `Particle.publish` function. `Particle.publish` takes two parameters. The first is the unique name of the event to publish, and the second is the data to be sent as part of the event.

Now you can flash the code to the Photon P1 using the Flash button in the Web IDE.

Let us go ahead and implement the code for Photon P2.

Create a new application in Particle Build with any name you want. You should now initialize a variable for the LED pin, and set it to output mode. Also, subscribe to the event. To do this, write the following code in the editing area:

```
// Set the LEDPin variable to the D7 digital I/O pin
int LEDPin = D7;

void setup() {

  // Set the pin D7 to output mode
  pinMode( LEDPin, OUTPUT );

  // Subscribe to the 'motion_alert' event and associate
  // the callback function 'eventHandler' with the event
  Particle.subscribe( "motion_alert", eventHandler);
}
```

By using the `Particle.subscribe` function, what we're saying is that each time the `motion_alert` event is received by Photon P2, the function named `eventHandler` should get executed.

Let us go ahead and implement the `eventHandler` function. The function takes in two parameters: the first is the name of the event, and the second is the data which is passed with it:

```
void eventHandler(const char *event, const char *data) {

  // check if message is "on"
  if ( strcmp ( data, "on" ) == 0 ) {

    // turn ON pin D7, hence the LED
    digitalWrite ( LEDPin, HIGH );

  } else if ( strcmp ( data, "off" ) == 0 ) {
```

```
    // turn OFF pin D7, hence the LED
    digitalWrite(LEDPin, LOW);
  }
}
```

In the preceding code, we cannot directly compare strings as we do with numbers, using the == operator; we need to use the strcmp function which takes in two string parameters to compare and returns a number. If 0 is returned, it means the specified strings are equal. On receiving the "on" message from the event, we turn On the LED. On receiving the "off" message, we switch Off the LED.

Photon with the RFID reader

RFID tags are usually fixed to objects, and are used to identify objects digitally. In our project, we don't need the objects. We will imagine that the RFID tags we have are attached to products, and are mapped to these products that are stored and used in the kitchen. To read the RFID tags, we use the RFID-RC522 RFID reader module connected to a Photon (P1). When the reader scans a tag (product), the data that is generated by the reader is sent to P1 through the wire. P1 then sends this product information as a message to the other Photon (P2), which has a motion sensor connected to it. Once the motion sensor senses motion, P2 relays the information (motion) to P1, which, in turn, posts the consolidated data to the remote database. The information in the database can be used later to monitor various products, and their movements, and perform various analyses.

The RFID-RC522 RFID reader has to be connected, as shown in *Figure 3*, to Photon P1, and the motion sensor has to be connected to Photon P2, as shown in *Figure 5*. Make sure that both the Photons have access to the Internet and are connected to Particle Build. To access RFID-RC522 from your code, you need to use a library. The library we're going to use is available at https://github.com/pkourany/MFRC522_RFID_Library. For the Photon P1, create a new app in the Web IDE, and name it p1_rfid. This will add a p1_rfid.ino file to your project automatically. Create a set of new tabs by clicking on the + button in the top-right corner of the Web IDE to create two new files, and name the files MFRC522.h and MFRC522.cpp. Get the code for these files from https://github.com/pkourany/MFRC522_RFID_Library, and paste their content into the corresponding new files and save them.

Now let us go ahead and add the code for the Photon P1, which will send out an event when the RFID reader reads a valid RFID tag:

```
// Program: Photon P1: RFID Reader
//--------------------------------------------------

// Include the library necessary to use the RFID reader
#include "MFRC522.h"

// define some constants
#define SS_PIN SS
#define RST_PIN D2

// Create an instance of the reader object
MFRC522 mfrc422(SS_PIN,RST_PIN);

// The setup() function gets called once when the device starts
void setup() {

  Serial.begin(9600);

  // Setup SPI configuration for communication to RFID reader
  mfrc522.setSPIConfig();

  // Initialize the RFID reader library
  mfrc522.PCD_Init();

  // Subscribe to the event generated from Photon P2
  // This event is generated when P2 detects motion
  Particle.subscribe("photon_rfid_moved", eventHandler);
}
```

In the setup() function, we first open the serial communication on port 9600. Next we set some default values for the RFID reader, and initialize it by executing the library's inbuilt functions, setSPIConfig() and PCD_Init(). We then subscribe to the event photon_rfid_moved, and map it to the function eventHandler whenever this event occurs. We continue with our code for P1 as follows:

```
// Code in this loop() function executes repeatedly, forever
void loop() {

  // If a new card isn't in scanning range, go back to
  // the beginning of the loop
  if ( !mfrc522.PICC_IsNewCardPresent()) {
    return;
```

```
  }

  // If a RFID tag serial number isn't read, go back and repeat
  if ( !mfrc522.PICC_ReadCardSerial()) {
    return;
  }

  // If we are here, a tag was detected.
  // Read the serial number of the tag as a character array
  char *uid = generateRFIDToChar(mfrc522.uid);
  // Send the serial number as a message to the Photon P2
  Particle.publish("photon_rfid_completed", String(uid));
}
```

In the preceding `loop()` function, we repeatedly check if an RFID tag is detected on the reader. On detecting one, we read its serial number by generating the string representation of the RFID UID (unique identifier). We then publish an event with the serial number so that Photon P2 can receive this message and map it to a motion sensor that may be triggered subsequently (of before), and the database can be updated accordingly. We still have to define the `eventHandler()` and `generateRFIDToChar()` functions. These are listed next:

```
  // This function is called when this Photon (P1)
  // receives a 'photon_rfid_moved' event
  void eventHandler(const char *event, const char *data) {

    // Read an RFID tag and send it to the cloud storage
    while(!mfrc522.PICC_IsNewCardPresent()) {
      char *rf_uid = generateRFIDToChar(mfrc522.uid);
      Particle.publish("post_to_db", String(rf_uid), 60, PRIVATE);
    }
  }
  // This function converts the Uid object returned by the library
  // to a char array
  Char *generateRFIDToChar(Uid *uid) {
    char result[uid->size];
    for (byte i=0; i < uid->size; i++) {
      result[i] = (uid->uidByte[i],HEX);
    }
    return result;
  }
  // End of Program: Photon 1
```

In the preceding code, once an event is received from Photon P2 about which motion sensor was triggered, Photon P1 publishes a message to the cloud storage to make a database entry with the given RFID tag and the timestamp.

Photon with the motion sensor

Now, let us go ahead and implement the code for Photon P2, which is connected to a motion sensor, listens for events from Photon P1, and generates events for P1.

Create a new application on Particle Build named `p2_motion_sensor`, and add the following code:

```
// Program: Photon P2: Motion Sensor
//-----------------------------------------------------

// Initialize some variables we'll need
int motionSensorPin = A0;
int sensorValue;
int previousSensorValue;
int MOVED_THRESHOLD = 4000;
int shelfNumber = 1;

// Do one-time setup
void setup() {

  // Setup pin A0 as an INPUT
  pinMode(motionSensorPin, INPUT);
  // Trigger a function called 'eventHandler' is a message
  // 'post_to_db' is received
  Particle.subscribe("post_to_db", eventHandler);
}
```

In the preceding code, we use the analog pin A0 for getting the input from the motion sensor. In this project, we have connected only one motion sensor to P2. For more advanced monitoring, multiple motion sensors can be connected to Photon P2, and it can be made to listen to all of them simultaneously. Once P2 has identified the source of movement, it can push that data to the cloud database. We also subscribe to the event `post_to_db`, which is generated from photon P1. This event tells P2 that a new object has been scanned, and it waits till some movement is registered on one of the motion sensors. We continue with the code for P2 as follows:

```
// Do the following repeatedly
void loop() {

  // Save the old sensor value
  int previousSensorValue = sensorValue;

  // Get the current sensor value by reading the A0 pin
  int sensorValue = analogRead(motionSensorPin);
  // Wait 1000 milliseconds (1 second) before repeating the loop
```

```
      delay(1000);
   }
```

In the `loop` function, we just store the current sensor value and the previous sensor value, and wait for one second before resuming the loop.

We will now implement the `eventHandler` function which is executed in P2 when a `post_to_db` event is received from P1:

```
// This function is executed when the post_to_db event is received
void eventHandler(const char *event, const char *data) {
    // Wait here as long as the sensorvalue is not greater than
    // the threshold
    while(!sensorValue > MOVED_THRESHOLD);
    // build the JSON String that is to be sent as payload with
    // the post_to_firebase_db event
    String msg = "{ "RFID" : " + String(data);
    msg += ", "SHELF_NO" : " + String(shelfNumber);
    msg += ", "TIMESTAMP" : "" + Time.timeStr() + "" }";

    // Send the JSON as a post_to_firebase_db event
    Particle.publish("post_to_firebase_db", msg, PRIVATE);
}
```

The `eventHandler` function waits until P2 senses motion. In this scenario, we assume that the motion is due to an RFID tagged item being kept on the shelf. Once motion is detected, P2 sends the information as a `post_to_firebase_db` event. This event is received by P1.

P1 then executes the webhook to post the data to the cloud database. The RFID tag serial number and the shelf number in which motion was detected are sent to the webhook, which posts the data to the cloud database.

In the next section, we discuss how to create a webhook to store data on the cloud database.

Data storage on the cloud

We use Firebase (`https://www.firebase.com`) for storing data on the cloud. Firebase is a backend-as-a-service provider which provides REST endpoints for data storage. We create webhooks to the Firebase REST endpoints to push data from the Photon to the cloud. We will pass the data to be stored in the `Particle.publish()` function at the time of invocation of the webhook event.

The following screenshot shows **Firebase** project creation screen:

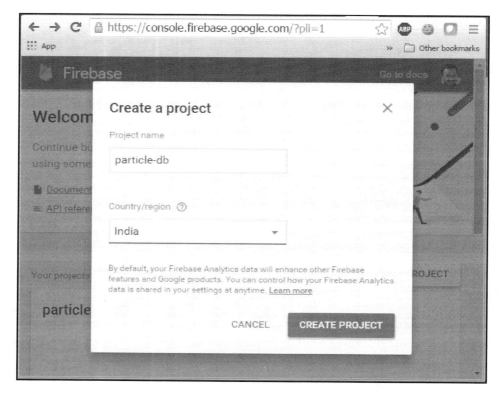

Figure 8: Project creation in firebase.com

We need to create a project in Firebase, but first we need to create an account at firebase.com. Point your browser to `https://www.firebase.com`, and create an account if you don't already have one. After the login/signup process, go ahead and create a new project as shown in *Figure 8*. Give a unique name to your Firebase project, and Firebase will generate a unique URL for your project upon creation, as highlighted in *Figure 9*. Keep the URL handy, as we will need it to create the webhook:

Figure 9: Firebase project URL

As seen in `Chapter 2`, *Fire Up Your Kit*, webhooks can be configured using the Particle dashboard (`https://dashboard.particle.io`). We will use this to set up our webhook.

Log in to your Particle dashboard, and select the Integrations (⁎) tab on the left tab pane. Click on New Integration (◉), then choose webhook (⚙) on the next screen. This brings up the webhook builder screen.

Fill in the webhook builder information, as follows, to create the webhook:

In the **Event Name** field, enter `post_to_firebase_db`, as we have used this name in our code. In the **URL** field, enter the URL generated and displayed in your Firebase console. Append `/inventory.json` to the URL you entered, as shown in the following screenshot. In the **Request Type** drop-down menu, select **POST**. In the **Device** drop-down list, select your device.

The following screenshot shows the required details that needs to be entered in their respective fields:

Figure 10: Particle webhook builder

In the **Advanced Settings** section of the webhook builder, we configure the **Send Custom Data** subsection with the template for the custom data we will be sending to Firebase. Enter the following in this subsection after selecting the **JSON** radio button, as shown in *Figure 10*:

```
{
   "RFID":"{{RFID_TAG}}",
   "SHELF_NO":"{{SHELF_NO}}",
   "TIMESTAMP":"{{PARTICLE_PUBLISHED_AT}}"
}
```

In the preceding template, the "{{ }}" signifies a variable value placeholder.

The **Webhook Reponses** subsection under **Advanced Settings** is used when the endpoint has to return some data which our code needs to use. The **Response Topic** option is to be filled with the name of the event we are subscribing to in our code.

Save the webhook by clicking on the **CREATE WEBHOOK** button.

Cloud data analysis and SMS notification

In the Firebase data store, we store the item ID, the timestamp of storing the item inside a kitchen cabinet, and the latest timestamp when it was taken out. The ID of the cabinet is also recorded to keep track of the location of storage. As soon as an event of storing or taking out an item occurs, a quick data analysis is performed, and an SMS is sent to alert the user if the inventory needs attention.

For the purposes of this project, the SMS can be sent using third-party service providers that work over the Internet. **Twilio** (https://www.twilio.com) provides a REST API using which our Photon can send SMS to users. The integration of Twilio with the Photon is done using webhooks, and the webhook event is triggered by the Photon using `Particle.publish()`.

The following is a list of some use cases which can be implemented by modifying the code in the previous sections:

- Send an SMS notification to the user whenever a new item is placed on the shelf.
- Send an SMS if an item is brought into the kitchen in spite of there being a bunch of similar items already present in the kitchen. The alert advises the user not to buy more, and to consume the old ones first.

- Send an SMS if an item is stored in the wrong cabinet. Each cabinet is designated for a certain group of items to enable efficient inventory management and safe storage. If the data storage analysis shows the item being stored in the wrong cabinet, it sends an alert to the user.

- Send an SMS alert to dispose of expired items, this requires additional data to be captured in the cloud storage, such as the expiry date of each product being scanned.

- Send an SMS advising the user to consume unused products before they expire.

- Send e-mails to the user with recommendations for similar items to buy by integrating with online grocery portals.

- Suggest new recipe ideas based on the items being taken out of the cabinets together.

- Alert to restock an item based on the stock count and its frequency of consumption.

We encourage you to try out some of these ideas, and implement a more advanced inventory system.

Troubleshooting

A real-life implementation of smart inventory management can have many challenges just like any typical wireless ad hoc sensor networks. Here, we highlight a few of the challenges you might face to make your project experience almost glitch free:

1. When there are multiple motion sensors and multiple RFID tags all working together, messages don't transmit reliably due to a high load on the network infrastructure (routers, network switches, and so on) as well as the microcontrollers and servers, causing packet drops. To troubleshoot such issues, a programmer should have a thorough understanding of the network environment, and the messaging software should be set up with the right values for parameters like QoS.

2. Most IoT devices use sensors at remote locations, and run on batteries, since an AC outlet may not be available where the sensing is done. In this scenario, it makes sense to select devices and write code so as to minimize the usage of power. This can be done by studying the specifications of the boards you plan to use and the programming API available for low-power modes of these boards.

3. Keep in mind that more sensors mean more battery power drainage, as typically, the sensors too run on batteries which are shared with the IoT board.

4. Monitoring the movement of an item in the warehouse correctly needs careful synchronization of actions that lead to data collection. If multiple processors (Photons) are deployed at different locations of the warehouse, monitoring different aspects of an item using different sensors, it becomes important to keep track of the sequence of events for the same item. If there are multiple item movements happening simultaneously, and only a handful of processors are multitasking to track all the items individually, a more advanced synchronization logic should be applied to ensure data correctness. Delay in sensor readings and unreliable wireless data communication medium adds to this challenge.

5. In RFID reader to Photon SPI interface, the SPI signal transmission is very high-speed, but effective over short distances only. To ensure reliable data exchange, SPI should be used to send data over distances no more than a few feet. Otherwise, you may get unreliable results, and debugging in this case becomes very challenging, as these kinds of failures are silent and sometimes intermittent and non-repeatable. If you notice some discrepancies, you can use advanced analyzers like the Saleae USB Logic Analyzer (https://www.saleae.com/), which can decode the transmitted data bytes and log them to a computer for further analysis.

6. In webhooks, the data from the Photon is pushed to the cloud by webhooks, which have some limitations on usage. As per the documentation provided by Particle at https://docs.particle.io/guide/tools-and-features/webhooks/#limits, Particle webhooks will not contact any host more often than 120 times per minute, and each user can create up to 20 webhooks, and can send 10 webhooks per minute, per device. There is also an error limit where a webhook will be disabled if a server returns an HTTP status code of 400 or greater, 10 times in a row. There is good reason for these limits as described on the linked page mentioned previously. It helps to be mindful of these.

7. In data streaming and offline storage, due to the restriction of the number of requests per minute, we cannot stream data in real time to/from any service. This can be worked around by aggregating multiple instances of data on the Photon for a predefined length of time, and then doing a bulk upload of the aggregated data to the server by sending a single webhook. With this approach, you can provide the data generated by the Photon in near real time. An important thing to keep in mind is that the memory in the Photon is limited, and the bulk upload per unit time has to be decided based on the memory requirements of the data.

Summary

The aim of this chapter was to introduce you to the world of warehouse management using different sensors, and usage of a cloud-based data store. The chapter talked about the challenges of setting up an IoT environment and a project setup. There are innumerable tools, both software and hardware, out there in the market, so a programmer needs to have the acumen to choose the right one. Experiencing and troubleshooting these types of challenges trains a programmer to select the right protocols and tools for a given project requirement, and to build more advanced projects.

This chapter focused on the communication aspect of a Photon. We demonstrated the communication between two or more Photons using the publisher/subscriber model, where one device communicates with the other device by generating events and passing data. We also discussed communication between a Photon and Internet-based services using webhooks.

In the next chapter, we will use the key concepts covered in this chapter to build an Internet-connected model car using a Photon.

5
Of Cars and Controllers

In this chapter, you are going to build a connected model car that can be controlled remotely. We will show you how this can be done by using the Photon as well as the Electron. We will demonstrate remote control of the model car using a computer keyboard as well as a Leap Motion (https://www.leapmotion.com/) controller.

We will begin with a discussion about the components to be used to build the model car, and how they should be connected and assembled together. We will use the local server setup from the *Local Server Setup* section in Chapter 3, *P2P and Local Server*, and plug in our code for controlling the car.

Towards the end of this chapter, we will explore an idea for hand-gesture control of the car using a Leap Motion controller.

This chapter covers the following topics:

- Building the model car – hardware components
- Building the model car – prerequisites
- Putting it all together and controlling the car
- Moving the car with gestures
- Programming the car with the Electron
- Troubleshooting

Building the model car – hardware components

In this section, we will build a model car from scratch, but first, we will list the hardware required.

The following is a list of hardware components, with their required quantities, which are needed to build the model car:

- Wheels (4)
- L293D motor driver (1)
- 65 Revolutions per minute (RPM) DC Right Angled motors (2)
- Chassis (1)
- Photon (1)
- Li-Po battery (1)
- 3-6V DC power supply (1)
- Jumper wires (a few)
- Breadboard (1)

The following is a brief description of some of these components:

Wheels

These could be any model car wheels suitable for use with DC motors. The ones we used for our project look like the ones shown in the following image:

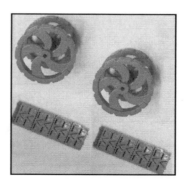

Figure 1: Wheels

L293D motor driver

L293D is an **Integrated Circuit (IC)** which is used to drive **direct current (DC)** motors. It is capable of driving the motors in either direction. It is a 16-pin IC, as shown in the following image:

Figure 2: L293D motor driver IC

This motor driver can simultaneously and independently control a set of two DC motors. The following diagram shows the pinout of the L293D motor driver IC:

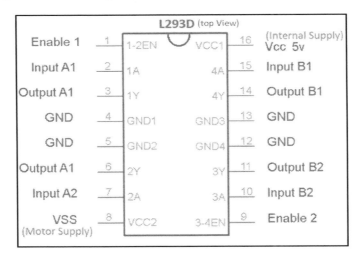

Figure 3: L293D motor driver pinout

The preceding figure shows the pin diagram of **L293D**. Pin **1** and pin **9** are enable pins for the left part and right part of the IC respectively, and must be set to HIGH for both parts of the IC to function. There are four input pins and four output pins, two on either side of the IC. The input pins are **2**, **7**, **10**, and **15**, and the corresponding output pins are **3**, **6**, **11**, and **14**. The IC needs a 5V power supply (it can go up to 36V) for its functioning, and this is supplied at the **Vcc** pin **16**. The power from pin **16** is not used to drive the motor, but only for making the IC function. Power for the motor has to be supplied via the **VSS** pin **8** in the range of 4.5V to 36V, depending upon the voltage rating of the motors you're using.

65 RPM DC Right Angled motor

Motors are the hardware components which actually drive the wheel. The input of the motor is to be connected to the output pins of the L293D motor driver. The Right Angled motors help in easy placement and fastening of the motors on the chassis. The following image shows such a motor:

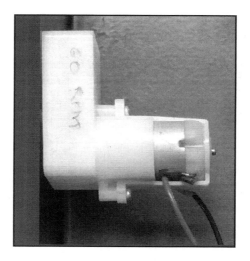

Figure 4: 65 RPM DC Right Angled motor

The motors require a voltage of 3V to 6V, and they draw a current of 200 mA each. The motors can drive the wheels at a speed of 65 RPM.

Chassis

A chassis is simply the frame onto which the motors and wheels are mounted. The following image shows a simple chassis with the motors fastened to it:

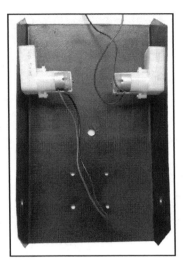

Figure 5: Chassis with motors

Power supply and Li-Po battery

A power supply of 3-6V is used to power the motors and the motor driver. The Li-Po battery is used to power the Photon which will enable intelligence for the model car. The alternative to using a Li-Po battery is using a 5V battery power bank which is commonly used to charge mobile devices.

Breadboard and jumper wires

The Breadboard is the canvas that an electronics hobbyist uses for prototyping a project. It allows you to place and connect the electronic components together as per a circuit diagram. There is no soldering needed to make the connections between multiple electronic components. They are connected together by simply inserting them directly onto the breadboard. You can also use jumper wires on the breadboard, just like components. The breadboard is reusable, and proves quite useful when prototyping projects.

The following image shows a breadboard:

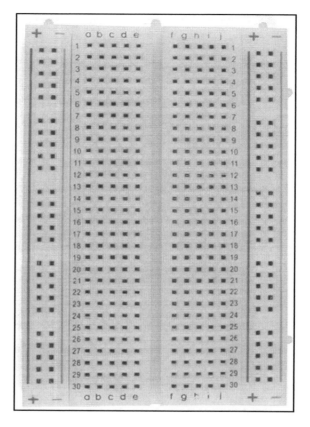

Figure 6: Breadboard

For building most of the circuits in this book, we need male-to-male jumper wires. These are easy to hook up on the breadboard. The following image shows male-to-male jumper wires:

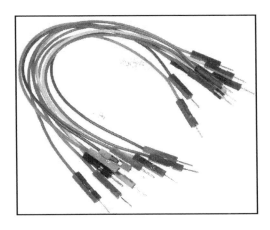

Figure 7: Male-to-male jumper wires

Building the model car – prerequisites

Now that you know what each of the hardware components do, we will see how we can put everything together and get the car moving by pressing the keys on your computer's keyboard. As a prerequisite, you need access to a computer, and you should set up a local P2P network using your computer. The Photon should be flashed with the **VoodooSpark** (h ttps://github.com/voodootikigod/voodoospark) firmware. This is covered in the *Setting up a P2P network for Particle devices* section in Chapter 3, *P2P and Local Server*. Before you set out to write the code, make sure you have assembled the car, and have connected the various hardware components as described in the previous section.

Putting it all together and controlling the car

Once the prerequisites are in place, you can start assembling the model car. First of all, fasten the motors to the chassis, one on each side of either the front or back side of the car, with the provided screws and clamps. The motors should appear to be driving the same axle. Next, attach a wheel to each of the two DC motor shafts; now attach the two remaining wheels to the non-motorized (imaginary) axle of the car.

Place the breadboard inside the chassis of the car, and assemble the Photon, the L293D motor driver IC, the Li-Po battery, and the 3-6V DC power supply on the breadboard. Now you should make the connections using the jumper wires as per the following connection diagram:

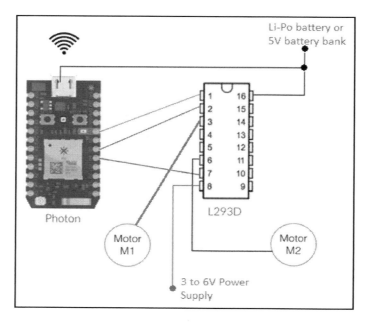

Figure 8: Photon to motor driver connection diagram

In this connection diagram, the **ground (GND)** connections are omitted for clarity. In actual practice, all GND pins need to be connected together, and this common ground point needs to be connected to the negative terminal of the power supply. The power supply inputs shown in the connection diagram are to be connected to the positive terminals of the respective power sources.

The Photon has seven digital output pins, and we utilize three of those pins for making the car move:

1. We connect the Photon's digital output **D7** to the L293D enable pin **1**. This will allow us to activate or deactivate the driver for both motors.
2. The Photon's digital output **D5** is connected to the L293D's A1 input pin **2**. The A1 input controls the left wheel.
3. Similarly, the Photon's digital output **D4** is connected to the L293D's A2 input pin **7**. The A2 input controls the right wheel.

4. The **Motor M1** (left) is connected to the L293D's A1 output pin **3**.

5. The **Motor M2** (right) is connected to the L293D's A2 output pin **6**.

It is assumed that the Photon is connected to a Wi-Fi network, and there is a proper power supply to both the Photon and the L293D driver IC.

The code

The code for moving the car using the keyboard relies on the Node.js modules—paricle-io and cylon. For installation of the required modules, refer to the *Setting up a P2P network for Particle devices* section in `Chapter 3`, *P2P and Local Server*.

The code sample we are going to describe is based on the assumption that you have set up the circuit on the breadboard as per the schematic diagram. You're encouraged to experiment with different modes of operation and see how it affects the movement of car. The logic to move the car is very simple: whenever the car is to be moved, both the DC motors should be powered and activated so they start rotating. This means the corresponding enable lines should be made HIGH.

At command prompt, create a new directory for this project, and change to it by running the following command:

```
$ mkdir car-project && cd car-project
```

Now you can create the Javascript file which will have the program implementation of this project. Using your favorite IDE or text editor, create a new file called `car.js`, and copy the following code into it:

```
// Program: Remote-Controlled Model Car
// -----------------------------------------------

// import the required libraries
var Particle = require('particle-io');
var Cylon = require('cylon');

// Initialize the board
var board = new Particle({
  token: process.env.PARTICLE_TOKEN,
  deviceId: process.env.PARTICLE_DEVICE_ID
});
```

In the preceding partial code, we create the Particle board object variable named `board`. The board object needs the token and device ID to connect with the Particle device, so we initialize it with these values stored in the environment variables `PARTICLE_TOKEN` and `PARTICLE_DEVICE_ID` respectively.

In case you want to hardcode these values instead of setting environment variables and using them, you can modify the previous code by replacing `process.env.PARTICLE_TOKEN` and `process.env.PARTICLE_DEVICE_ID` with actual values.

Continuing our code, we add an event handler on the board object for the `ready` event, which is emitted when the connection has been established with the Photon:

```
// Add an event handler for the 'ready' event
board.on("ready", function(){
  // This is the body of the callback function of this
  // event. Code written here gets executed when we are
  // connected to the board
});
```

We will now add our logic to the handler's callback function. This code will get executed when the `ready` event is triggered.

Add the following code inside the body of the callback function:

```
// Initialize required variables
var analogValue = 0;
var digitalValue = 0;
var moving = false;
var breadBoard = this;

// Setup digital pins D4, D5 and D7 as OUTPUT pins
this.pinMode("D4",this.MODES.OUTPUT);
this.pinMode("D5",this.MODES.OUTPUT);
this.pinMode("D7", this.MODES.OUTPUT);

// Set the output of these pins to the current value (0) of
// the digitalValue variable.
this.digitalWrite("D4",digitalValue);
this.digitalWrite("D5",digitalValue);
this.digitalWrite("D7",digitalValue);
```

We initialize the variables `analogValue`, `digitalValue`, `moving`, and `breadBoard` to the default values.

The `this` keyword refers to the current object, and in this case, it refers to the board object.

The `pinMode()` function sets a pin to the specified mode (`INPUT` or `OUTPUT`). In the `INPUT` mode, the Photon can sense external input via the pin setup in the `OUTPUT` mode, and the resulting event can be used to trigger actions. In the `OUTPUT` mode, the Photon can send out data to other devices or sensors in the form of a HIGH or LOW signal from the pin setup in the `OUTPUT` mode.

Next we set the pins `D4`, `D5`, and `D7` to default values using the `digitalWrite()` function, which takes in two input parameters—the pin number to output the value to, and the value to be written (HIGH or LOW).

In the subsection *Controlling your Particle board using the keyboard* of `Chapter 3`, *P2P and Local Server*, we introduced you to a Javascript library called **Cylon.js** which facilitates the connection between various hardware devices. We will use this library to listen for keyboard events. These events can then be used to move the car around.

Continuing the code, we have the following:

```
// Setup or initialize the Cylon object with the
// connection details, device details and work function
Cylon.robot({
  connections: {
    keyboard: {adaptor: 'keyboard'},
  },
  devices: {
    keyboard: {driver: 'keyboard'},
  },
  work: function(my){
    // The logic of moving the car goes here
  }

}).start();
```

The preceding code is the boilerplate code for working with Cylon.js. The `robot()` function takes in a dictionary of parameters with the following three mandatory keys:

- **Connections**: A dictionary of the hardware devices to be connected and their corresponding adaptor.
- **Devices**: A dictionary in which the hardware is mapped to the driver to be used with the given hardware.
- **Work**: A user-defined function which should be executed on the given hardware. The function takes in the current Cylon object as parameter, using which the hardware can be accessed in code.

Now, we will go ahead and add the logic to control the car via the keyboard. The logic will be implemented inside the `work` function, so make sure you put the following code inside the `work` function block:

```
// Listen for the "up" keystroke and
// Start moving the car if the 'up' key is pressed
my.keyboard.on('up', function(){

    // set variables to appropriate values
    moving = true;
    analogValue = 255;
    digitalValue = 1;

    // Set D4, D5 and D7 HIGH so that the motors are
    // enabled and the car starts moving
    breadBoard.digitalWrite("D7",1);
    breadBoard.digitalWrite("D4",1);
    breadBoard.digitalWrite("D5",1);
});

// Listen for the "down" keystroke and
// Stop moving the car if the 'down' key is pressed
my.keyboard.on('down', function(){

    // set variables to appropriate values
    moving = false;
    analogValue = 0;
    digitalValue = 0;

    // Set D4, D5 and D7 LOW so that the motors are
    // disabled and the car stops moving
    breadBoard.digitalWrite("D4",0);
    breadBoard.digitalWrite("D5",0);
    breadBoard.digitalWrite("D7",0);
});

// End of Program: Remote-Controlled Model Car
//-------------------------------------------------
```

In the preceding code listing, we added two event handlers on the keyboard. Whenever the up button on the keyboard is pressed, the corresponding handler's callback function executes, and the car starts to move forward. The code in this callback function activates the L293D by sending a HIGH signal to its **Enable 1** (pin 1), and HIGH signals are sent to its **Input A1** (pin 2) and **Input A2** (pin 7), which drive the DC motors.

Similarly, another event handler is added on the down button to stop the moving car once the down button is pressed. We send a LOW signal to the same pins to deactivate the L293D, stopping the DC motors, thus bringing the car to a halt.

This completes the code for our remote-controlled model car.

Running the program and controlling the car

To start the program, execute the following in a command window after making sure you are in the project directory:

```
$ node car.js
```

Once the program starts, you can press the up key on the keyboard to start moving the car forward. Pressing the down key stops the car.

Congratulations! You have built your remote-controlled model car using a P2P network and sending control signals via your keyboard.

The following image shows the fully assembled remote-controlled model car:

Figure 9: Model car, fully assembled

Moving the car with gestures

It would be interesting to be able to move the model car with hand gestures. In this section, we explore the possibilities of the same. An additional piece of hardware is needed to track hand movements or gestures and convert them to events that our code can use. We can use a Leap Motion (`https://www.leapmotion.com/`) controller for this purpose. The Leap Motion controller uses two monochromatic infrared cameras and three infrared LEDs. The device can track up to 10 fingers in real time, and transmit the data to a computer using USB.

The following image shows a Leap Motion controller in use:

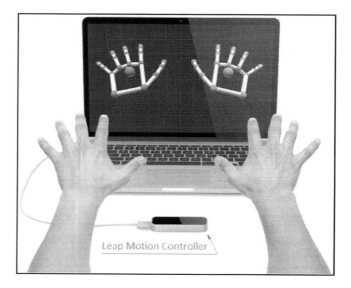

Figure 10: Leap Motion controller

How it works

We use the spherical radius of palm output parameter of the Leap Motion controller as the input which drives the model car. We do this by continuously monitoring the spherical radius value as seen by the controller. When the palm of your hand is stretched, that is, the spherical radius is large, the car starts moving, and when the palm is closed (when the spherical radius is small), the car comes to a halt.

The logic for the movements of the car can be borrowed from the previous section. Just like we did with the keyboard, a Leap Motion controller is connected to the network using the Cylon.js library. We use the same boilerplate code for Cylon.js, and just modify the parameters to make it work with the Leap Motion controller. Before writing the following Node.js code, you should make sure you have the Leap Motion drivers installed on your computer.

The code

Using a text editor, edit the `car.js` file, and modify the `Cylon.robot()` function as follows:

```
// Setup or initialize the Cylon object with the
// connection details, device details and work function
Cylon.robot({
  connections: {
    leapmotion: { adaptor: 'leapmotion' }
  },

  devices: {
    leapmotion: { driver: 'leapmotion' }
  },

  work: function(my) {

    // Listen for the 'hand' event
    my.leapmotion.on('hand', function(payload){

      // Get the 'spherical radius' of the hand
      var radius = payload.sphereRadius;

      // Turn off the outputs to stop the car when the
      // radius is below a threshold
      if (radius <= 40){
        moving = false;
        analogValue = 0;
        digitalValue = 0;
        that.digitalWrite("D4",0);
        that.digitalWrite("D5",0);
        that.digitalWrite("D7",0);
      }
      else

      // Turn ON the outputs to start the car when the
      // radius is above the threshold
```

```
        {
          moving = true;
          digitalValue = 1;
          analogValue = ( radius - 40 ) * 0.7084;
          that.digitalWrite("D7",1);
          that.digitalWrite("D4",1);
          that.digitalWrite("D5",0);
        }
      });
    }
  }).start();
```

The Leap Motion controller emits the `'hand'` event whenever it notices a hand hovering over it. The event handler's callback function has one object parameter called `payload`, which has a field called `sphereRadius` among others. According to our observations, the value of `sphereRadius` is less than `40` when the palm is closed, and it is above `40` when the palm is open. We use this variation to decide whether to move the car or not. Obviously, this figure of `40` can vary from person to person. So the `sphereRadius` threshold should be adjusted by performing some trials. You can log the value of `sphereRadius` to see what value fits your case. Typically, the value lies between 40 and 50.

To run the code, follow the steps described in the earlier section. You should now be able to move and stop your connected car with hand gestures!

Programming the car with the Electron

The Electron is a prototyping board from Particle which has a built-in GSM module. Using the GSM module, the Electron can connect to the internet using a 3G/2G network.

In the projects we have seen so far, the controller and the car are on the same Wi-Fi network. In this section, we explore a scenario where there is no common network between the controller and the model car that needs to be remote-controlled. How do we control the car remotely in this situation? We replace the Photon in the model car with the Electron. This allows the car to be in a completely different region and still be controllable remotely.

Putting it all together (again)

Connect the circuit as shown in the next schematic diagram. The connections are similar to the ones you did for the Photon-based projects. The Electron has to be connected to a Li-Po battery, which is included in the package when you buy the Electron. Make sure the battery is completely charged before mounting it with the Electron on the model car.

In this project, we will write some code on the Particle cloud in the Particle's Web IDE, and we will use the Particle mobile application (`https://play.google.com/store/apps/detai ls?id=io.particle.android.app`) to control the pins on the Electron, which, in turn, will control the model car.

The following diagram shows the connections between the Electron and the motor driver IC:

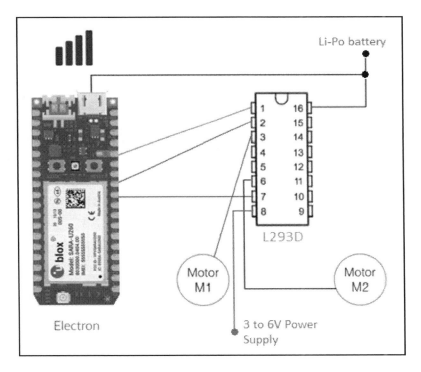

Figure 11: Electron to motor driver connection diagram

The code

Fire up your web browser, and point it to the Particle Web IDE at `https://build.particl`
`e.io`.

Create a new project, and add the following code to it:

```
// Program: Remote Control Model Car using Electron
//------------------------------------------------

// Initialize required variables
int enablePin = D7;
int input2Pin = D5;
int input7Pin = D4;

// Declare functions to stop and move the car
void stopCar();
void moveCar();

// Setup the pins to output mode and set them to 'LOW' so
// that the car is in stopped state when the program starts
void setup() {

  pinMode(enablePin, OUTPUT);
  pinMode(input2Pin, OUTPUT);
  pinMode(input7Pin, OUTPUT);

  digitalWrite(enablePin, LOW);
  digitalWrite(input2Pin, LOW);
  digitalWrite(input7Pin, LOW);

  Particle.function("stopCar", stopCar);
  Particle.function("moveCar", moveCar);
}

void loop() {
  //Do nothing in the loop
}
```

In the preceding code, we set the mode of operation of the digital pins D7, D5, and D4 to
OUTPUT. Pin D7 is the activation pin for the L293D driver, and pins D5 and D4 are inputs to
the motors. To move the car, set the pins in the following order: D4, D5, and then D7 to
HIGH. To bring the car to a halt, set D7 to LOW.

We also declared two functions, stopCar() and moveCar(), which we expose as APIs for
the client applications.

Continuing with the code, add the implementations of the `stopCar()` and `moveCar()` functions as follows:

```
// This function stops the car by setting the pins to LOW
void stopCar() {
  digitalWrite(input2Pin,LOW);
  digitalWrite(input7Pin,LOW);
  digitalWrite(enablePin,LOW);
}

// This function starts the car by setting the pins to HIGH
void moveCar() {
  digitalWrite(input2Pin,HIGH);
  digitalWrite(input7Pin,HIGH);
  digitalWrite(enablePin,HIGH);
}
```

Once this code is running, these functions can be executed remotely via the Internet by making `POST` requests to the following URLS:

- `https://api.particle.io/v1/devices/{DEVICE_ID}/stopCar`
- `https://api.particle.io /v1/devices/{DEVICE_ID}/moveCar`

In these URLs, `{DEVICE_ID}` needs to be replaced with the actual **Device ID** of your Electron. You can obtain **Device ID** from your Particle build dashboard by clicking on the

devices tab ( ) on the left, and then clicking on the **device**.

With the aforementioned URLs, you can build your own client application instead of using a mobile phone as a controller. For example, the client controller can be a web application or simply a cURL command from the command line.

Troubleshooting

The projects in this chapter require some physical assembly of parts. The electronic aspect is similar to the projects in earlier chapters of this book.

Common precautions to take and the pitfalls to watch out for while implementing these projects include the following:

- Make sure the VoodooSpark firmware is installed on your Photon and that it is functioning by building the example given in the *Setting up a P2P network for Particle devices* section in `Chapter 3`, *P2P and Local Server*.

- While connecting the L293D motor driver, watch out for correct pin numbering of this IC, where, unlike the Particle devices, pin numbers are not labelled. They need to be discerned from a reference dot or notch on the IC itself. If you are new to handling ICs, see `https://learn.sparkfun.com/tutorials/integrated-circuits#ic-packages` for information on how to find IC pin numbers.
- The Photon/Electron, L293D motor driver IC, and motors may be powered using different power sources. We normally connect the GND pins/terminals of each component to the negative terminal of its own power source. Make sure the negative terminals of all power sources are connected together to provide a common reference point for all voltages across the circuit.
- Make sure you use power sources of the correct voltages and current capabilities to power each component in the circuit.
- The Electron uses a SIM card to connect to the Internet using GPRS. Make sure the subscription for the SIM is valid, and the connectivity to the network is established.

Summary

This chapter takes many ideas discussed in `Chapter 3`, *P2P and Local Server*, and uses them to create a remote control model car. We began by listing the various hardware components needed to build the model car, and then moved on to the schematic of the circuit. We created a P2P network using the VoodooSpark firmware. We then created an event-based program to listen for certain events of the keyboard and perform actions. We saw how other hardware sensors can be brought into the network using Cylon.js. This was demonstrated by adding a Leap Motion controller to the network, and using it to control the car with gestures. At the end of the chapter, we added the Electron to the model car project in order to make the setup completely mobile and local-network independent. We also saw how we can add code to implement cloud functions and expose them as APIs, which can be used to create custom client-side applications to control the model car.

In the next chapter, you'll learn all about Particle firmware, how to modify firmware, and different ways of flashing your own firmware onto your Particle devices.

6
Hacking the Firmware

In this chapter, we will take a look at the firmware of the Photon and Electron devices from Particle. You will learn different ways of obtaining and deploying the firmware. You will also see how you can set up your local machine for building the firmware from source code and deploy it on your Particle devices. Finally, we will briefly touch upon the role of custom firmware for Particle devices.

The following topics are covered in this chapter:

- What is firmware?
- Obtaining and flashing firmware
- Custom firmware

What is firmware?

Firmware is the permanent software programmed into a read-only memory of a computing device. Firmware, which is usually added at the time of manufacturing, is necessary to run user programs on the device. The firmware software provides control, monitoring, and data manipulation of devices or products. Typical examples of devices containing firmware are embedded systems such as traffic lights, consumer appliances, remote controls, digital watches, computers, computer peripherals, mobile phones, and digital cameras. The firmware contained in these devices provides low-level control for the device. Firmware code persists across power cycles (switching on and off, and back on).

Firmware is held in non-volatile memory such as ROM, EPROM, or flash memory. Most firmware can be updated. Common reasons for updating firmware include fixing bugs or adding features to the device. This is usually done by reprogramming the flash memory through a special procedure. Firmware, such as the program of an embedded system, may be the only program running on the system, and provide all of its functions. Some devices such as Particle boards have separate areas for firmware and user programs. The user programs reside in flash memory, and can be easily updated.

For most consumer devices in the past, the firmware was nearly never updated, which meant no new features were added during the lifetime of the consumer device. This trend has changed dramatically over the course of the last few years. Google, with its Android operating system, introduced the concept of **Over-the-Air** (OTA) firmware updates, which essentially involved pushing the firmware updates over the Internet directly to the device. The functionality and lifetime of electronic devices have gone up in the last few years. This means that the hardware being released today is ahead of its time, and will last up to a few years in the future. To support new features, providing updates becomes crucial. Internet-connected devices have made it very simple to provide such updates with zero intervention from the user.

A bit of history

The term firmware was coined in 1967 to denote the contents of a writable control store, which is essentially the high-speed memory implementing the computer's instruction set. Initially, firmware contained low-level code, which helped in the implementation of machine instructions. Firmware acted as the interface between the hardware and the software. In the 1990s, updating firmware involved replacing the storage medium containing the firmware, usually a ROM chip. If something went wrong in the process, it would render the device unusable. The term **bricked** is used to refer to an electronic device that would not work due to firmware-related errors.

Obtaining and flashing firmware

Microcontrollers do not directly understand human-readable code. The firmware code is written in the C language by the programmer. This needs to be converted to a binary format that can be understood by the Particle microcontrollers. A program called a compiler does this conversion.

A local setup is required to be able to work with firmware. Such a setup provides you with all the software and packages needed to compile and deploy the firmware.

Flashing firmware involves two main steps:

1. Obtaining firmware.
2. Burning firmware onto the device.

Obtaining firmware

To be able to flash a firmware, we need to get the firmware file in binary format. There are two ways you can obtain the firmware:

* Direct download
* Building from source

Obtaining firmware by direct download

The easiest way to get the latest firmware is to download it from the firmware release page at `https://github.com/spark/firmware/releases/`.

At the time of writing of this book, the latest firmware available for Particle Photon and Spark Core is versioned at 0.5.2. Depending on your device, download the correct binary firmware file from the version-specific download page at `https://github.com/spark/firmware/releases/tag/v.5.2`. The download is provided in two parts. For the Photon, download the following files:

* `system-part1-0.5.2-photon.bin`
* `system-part2-0.5.2-photon.bin`

For Spark Core, download the following files:

* `system-part1-0.5.2-p1.bin`
* `system-part2-0.5.2-p1.bin`

Obtaining firmware by building from source

In this section, we will see how to get the latest firmware source code, and build it on our local machine. Before we can build the firmware code written in C on our local machine, we need to install certain tools and packages, and prepare our environment for action. We will now see how to install these on Linux, Mac, and Windows. We need the following to be installed and configured on our computer:

- **Compiler**: ARM GCC
- **Build tool**: Make
- **Version control system**: Git

ARM GCC

GCC is the compiler tool-chain for the C language. The Particle Photon/Core uses an ARM-based microcontroller. So we require the ARM variant of GCC. More specifically, the Particle firmware build requires ARM GCC version 4.9.3 20150529 or newer.

Installing ARM-GCC on Linux and Windows

The binaries of ARM GCC for Linux and Windows are available at `https://launchpad.net/gcc-arm-embedded`.

Download the appropriate binary, and install the same to get ARM GCC on your Linux or Windows system.

Installing ARM-GCC on Mac OS

Installing ARM GCC on Mac OS is done using Homebrew (`http://brew.sh/`). Use the instructions at the Homebrew web page to install Homebrew on your Mac. ARM GCC is maintained in Homebrew's PX4 module. If you are installing GCC for the first time, run the following command at your terminal to add the PX4 repository to the local `brew` database:

```
$ brew tap PX4/homebrew-PX4
```

Now run the following commands to update the local `brew` database, and install ARM GCC:

```
$ brew update
$ brew install gcc-arm-none-eabi-49
```

The preceding commands install GCC-ARM-49 on your local machine.

If you already have another version of ARM GCC installed using brew, and need to update the version, then run the following commands:

```
$ brew update
$ brew install gcc-arm-none-eabi-49      # install new required version
$ brew unlink gcc-arm-none-eabi-48       # Unlink the previous version
$ brew link --overwrite gcc-arm-none-eabi-49
```

Since we have two versions of ARM GCC installed on the Mac, we need to tell the computer explicitly to use the latest version by unlinking the older version. The preceding commands are an example of replacing the installed version (4.8) with a newer version (4.9) on your Mac machine.

You can check the current version of ARM GCC that will be used with the following command:

```
$ arm-none-eabi-gcc -version
```

Make

`make` is a command-line utility that compiles and builds binaries from source code by reading a configuration file called a makefile. A makefile specifies how to compile and generate the binary by following a list of commands.

Installing make on Linux and Mac

Linux and Mac OSes have `make` pre-installed, and we will be using this to build the firmware. Some Linux distributions may not bundle *make*. In this case, it can be installed with the following commands on Debian based systems:

```
$ sudo apt-get install build-essential   # on Debian-based systems
```

or, on Fedora/RedHat based systems, run the following command:

```
$ yum install make                       # on Fedora/RedHat based systems
```

Installing make on Microsoft Windows

Executable binaries for `make` are available at http://gnuwin32.sourceforge.net/packages/make.htm. Download the binary package on your local computer, unzip it, and run the executable provided to install `make`.

Git

Git is a distributed version control system. We need the Git client to access the firmware source code available from online Git repositories.

Installing Git on Microsoft Windows and Mac OS

The *Git* binaries for Windows and Mac OS are available at
`http://git-scm.com/download/win` and `http://git-scm.com/download/mac` respectively.

To install Git, download the appropriate package for your architecture (32-bit or 64-bit) and OS, and follow the instructions provided on the Git website.

Installing Git on Linux

On most Linux distributions, Git is available in the distribution's online repositories. This can be downloaded and installed using the distribution's package manager. To install `git` on Debian-based Linux systems, run the following commands in your terminal:

```
$ sudo apt-get update
$ sudo apt-get install git
```

Getting the firmware source code

All the dependencies required to build the firmware code are now installed on your local machine. Now let's grab the latest firmware source code from GitHub using the `git` command.

Open a terminal window, create a new directory, and change to it.

Now run the following command:

```
$ git clone https://github.com/spark/firmware
```

This preceding command will download the latest firmware code from GitHub into a new sub-directory, called firmware, in the current directory.

Compiling the code

We compile firmware code using the `make` command-line utility.

Navigate to the firmware/build directory, and get the common libraries needed to compile the code by running the following commands:

```
$ cd firmware/build
$ git clone https://github.com/spark/core-common-lib
```

Now navigate to the root folder of the firmware (the folder called `firmware`), and run the following command:

```
$ cd ..   # You should now be in the "firmware" folder containing the
makefile
$ make clean all
$ cd build
$ ./release-all.sh
```

The preceding commands will compile the firmware code, and create the binary file in the `firmware/build` folder. The newly built binary firmware file will be named `core-firmware.bin`.

Burning firmware onto the device

Firmware can be burnt to Particle devices in three ways:

- OTA
- Using Particle-CLI
- The DFU-Util method

Burning firmware using the OTA method

The OTA method works by pushing the firmware over the network to the Particle device by running commands on your local machine. You will need to obtain the firmware binary corresponding to your device by using one of the methods described in the previous section. Once you have the firmware binary files, navigate to the directory containing the firmware binaries using the command line:

```
$ cd absolute/path/to/binary/files
```

We assume that you have already installed `particle-cli`, the Particle command-line client, using instructions from *Software setup* in `Chapter 2`, *Fire Up Your Kit*. It is also assumed that the machine is connected to the device via Wi-Fi/USB. You need to have your Particle device name at the ready. This can be obtained by running the following at the command prompt:

```
$ particle list
```

The preceding command generates a list of devices you own, and displays a information about their status, variables, and functions. The output from running the command is given as follows:

```
Checking with the cloud...
Retrieving devices... (this might take a few seconds)
MY_DEVICE_NAME (0123456789ABCD) 0 variables, 0 functions
```

To flash the firmware to a Photon, run the following commands from your terminal or command prompt:

```
$ particle flash MY_DEVICE_NAME system-part1-0.5.2-photon.bin$ particle
flash MY_DEVICE_NAME system-part2-0.5.2-photon.bin
```

To flash firmware to a Spark Core, replace the file names in the preceding commands with the firmware binary filenames of Spark Core.

During the flashing process, your device's LED glows with different colors corresponding to the different codes. Initially, the LED should be cyan; as soon as you run the aforementioned commands, the LED should change its color to yellow, and then to magenta as the firmware is being flashed. Once the firmware is flashed successfully, the device will restart automatically, and try to connect to the configured Wi-Fi network.

Burning firmware using Particle-CLI

The method described here is the easiest, but this method only flashes firmware which have been released as a stable version. Using this method, you can flash the last stable firmware released for your device, but not the latest one. Using the stable version is good for large-scale deployments of devices. You will need to have the `particle-cli` tool installed on your machine.

To start flashing the firmware using this method, put the device in DFU-mode by following the steps given next:

1. Hold down both RST and MODE buttons of the device.
2. Release only the RST button while holding down the MODE button.
3. Wait for the LED to start flashing yellow.
4. Release the MODE button.

DFU mode is used to flash the firmware and programs from the local machine. It provides the fastest way to burn code on your Particle devices.

Run the following commands to update your device to the last stable firmware release. The first command updates `particle-cli` to the latest available stable version, and the second command downloads and flashes the firmware on to the device:

```
$ npm update -g particle-cli
$ particle update
```

Once the firmware is flashed successfully, the device will restart automatically and try to connect to the configured Wi-Fi network.

Burning firmware using the DFU-Util method

We will need the DFU-Util software (`http://dfu-Util.sourceforge.net/`) to be installed on the system to use this method. We will now see how to install it on Linux, Mac, and Windows.

Installing DFU-Util

DFU-Util is the implementation of specifications described in DFU 1.0 and DFU 1.1 of the USB forum. It is intended to download and upload firmware to/from devices, which range from micro-controller boards to mobile phones, connected over USB. You will be using DFU-Util to mostly push custom firmware. A DFU-Util can be installed on the Linux, Mac, and Windows Operating Systems.

Installing of DFU-Util on Linux

Most Linux distributions can get DFU-Util as binary packages downloadable from their online repositories. On major Linux distributions such as Debian, Ubuntu, and Fedora/Redhat, `dfu-util` can be installed through the distribution's package manager tools. For Ubuntu- and Debian-based systems, run the following command in a terminal:

```
$ sudo apt-get install dfu-util
```

For Fedora/Redhat-based distributions, run the following command in a terminal:

```
$ sudo yum install dfu-util
```

The package manager will fetch and install the required files and all the dependencies, and add the DFU-Util executables to your PATH so that they can be accessed at the terminal.

This makes your Linux system ready to use DFU-Util tp flash firmware to your Particle devices.

Installing of DFU-Util on Mac OS

Installing of DFU-Util on Mac OS is done using Homebrew (http://brew.sh/). If Brew is not installed already, use the instructions at the Homebrew web page to install it on your Mac.

Once Brew is installed on your Mac, run the following command on your terminal to install dfu-util:

```
$ brew install dfu-util
```

This makes the Mac system ready to use DFU-Util to flash firmware to your Particle devices.

Installing of DFU-Util on Microsoft Windows

On Windows, DFU-Util needs the Core DFU driver. The driver can be installed using Zadig (http://zadig.akeo.ie). Zadig is a Windows application that installs generic USB drivers. After installation of Zadig, execute the Zadig program and follow the instructions listed next:

1. Click on **Options | List all devices**.
2. In the drop-down list, select **CORE DFU** and **libusbK** for the driver. Press the **Install Driver** button.
3. You should see the message **The driver was installed successfully** after a short while.

For details of this installation, go to the following link: https://community.particle.io/t/tutorial-installing-dfu-driver-on-windows-24-feb-215/3518.

Now that the DFU-Util driver has been installed, we need to download the DFU-Util binaries and add them to the PATH variable so they can be accessed from any directory at the command line. DFU-Util can be downloaded from this link: https://s3.amazonaws.com/spark-assets/dfu-util-.8-binaries.tar.xz. Extract the files, and note down the location of the extracted files.

To add DFU-Util to your system PATH, perform the following steps:

1. Open system's **Control Panel**.
2. Click the **Advanced system settings** link.
3. Click on the **Environment Variables** button.

4. Under **System Variables**, select **Path** and click on **Edit**.

5. Add the absolute path of the DFU-Util binaries at the end of the path list. This path will be as follows: `<Extracted Folder>\win32-mingw32\`

6. `<Extracted Folder>` is the full path up to the `dfu-util-0.8-binaries` folder, which gets created when extracting the `*.tar.xz` file as mentioned earlier.

7. Save and close all dialog windows.

This makes the Windows system ready to use DFU-Util to flash firmware to your Particle devices.

Flashing firmware

Before firmware can be flashed, the Particle device has to be set to DFU mode as described in the *Burning firmware using Particle-CLI* section earlier.

Next, we need to get the memory address that the OS assigns to the USB-connected device. This can be obtained from the Windows Device Manager, or by running the following command:

```
$ dfu-util -1
```

The preceding command should print output similar to the following on the screen:

```
Found DFU: [1d50:607f] devnum=0, cfg=1, intf=0, alt=0, name="@Internal
Flash  /0x08000000/12*001Ka,116*001Kg"Found DFU: [1d50:607f] devnum=0,
cfg=1, intf=0, alt=1, name="@SPI Flash : SST25x/0x00000000/512*04Kg"
```

Note the value at the highlighted position. This is the USB address assigned to your device. This value could be different in your case. We will need to use this address in the firmware flash command.

To flash the downloaded firmware on the Photon, run the following commands:

```
$ dfu-util -d 1d50:607f -a 0 -s 0x8020000 -D system-part1-0.5.2-photon.bin$
dfu-util -d 1d50:607f -a 0 -s 0x8060000:leave -D system-part2-0.5.2-
photon.bin
```

Similarly, to flash the downloaded firmware on a Core, replace the `*.bin` filenames with the corresponding Core ones.

To flash the compiled firmware, run the following commands:

```
$ cd /path/to/firmware/build
$ dfu-util -d 1d50:607f -a 0 -s 0x08005000:leave -D core-firmware.bin
```

After a successful flash, the Particle device will automatically restart and connect to the configured Wi-Fi network.

Custom firmware

The stock firmware provided with Particle devices is good for prototyping but, when building a product for production, the firmware needs to be optimized for a particular function that the Particle device will need to perform over an extended period of time. Firmware that can cater to this need is called custom firmware.

Custom firmware is a modified version of the official firmware. This is usually created to enhance the features the device would otherwise have. You get Particle devices pre-programmed with an official firmware. This can be replaced with builds of the firmware modified to provide other functions and support for other types of programming. Often, when the hardware device has to be deployed for a specific use case in production, the firmware may need to be stripped down to the functionalities one actually needs, to free up memory, for example. With the official firmware, Particle supports programming in the C language. Sometimes, the programmer is skilled in a programming language that is not supported OTB. In both cases, customized firmware can potentially provide optimal functionality and better performance by freeing up memory, or supporting a programming language of the user's choice.

Thus, there is a need for developing custom firmware to address these requirements. The Particle team understood this need, and has provided an easy way to build and deploy custom firmware onto Particle devices. To this end, Particle has open-sourced its firmware code, and it has provided instructions to build the firmware at `https://github.com/spark/firmware/wiki` (See the links on the right panel.)

This means that, anyone with the necessary skills can modify the firmware code and rebuild a customized version of the firmware catering to specific requirements, as mentioned earlier.

An example of a custom firmware for Particle devices is **VoodooSpark** (`https://github.c om/voodootikigod/voodoospark`). VoodooSpark is a customized firmware build for Particle's Spark Core and Photon devices to allow a remote interface definition of the firmware API over a local TCP connection. This allows client-side programs to directly control the Particle devices in real time regardless of their programming language. For example, a Node.js program can drive the Particle devices by executing the firmware API-level commands dynamically.

Summary

In this chapter, you learnt to work with the firmware of Particle devices. You learnt different ways to obtain firmware and deploy it to the devices. We saw how to set up our local machine Linux, Mac, or Windows, for development and deployment of firmware from source code. Finally, we discussed the role of custom firmware for Particle devices.

Index

A

Access Point (AP) 19
ACCESS-TOKEN 54
Advanced Message Queuing Protocol (AMQP)
    reference link 63
alternate protocols, IoT
    about 62
    Constrained Application Protocol (CoAP) 63
    MQ Telemetry Transport (MQTT) 62
Arduino Tweet Library
    reference link 43
Authorization Bearer Token 38

B

binaries, ARM-GCC for Linux and Windows
    reference link 110
BitTorrent 52
burnt process 15

C

Central Processing Unit (CPU) 9
client-server architecture
    versus P2P architecture 53
    versus P2P network 51
cloud data
    analyzing 83
cloud services
    about 10
    Amazon Web Services 13
    AnyPresence 14
    Appcelerator 14
    Cloud Foundry 13
    IBM Bluemix 13
    Kinvey 14
    market survey 11
    Microsoft Azure 13

Parse 14
    ThingWorx 14
color codes
    reference link 28
Command Line Interface (CLI) 29
communication, between Photons
    about 72
    motion sensor, using 78
    RFID reader, using 75
    sample code 73
Concise Binary ObjecT Representation (CBOR) 63
Constrained Application Protocol (CoAP)
    reference link 63
Core
    about 16
    comparing, with Electron 20
    comparing, with Photon 20
    connecting 31
    setting up 28
cURL 54
custom firmware
    about 118
    reference link 118
Cylon-MQTT module 62
Cylon.js 97

D

data
    storing, on cloud 79
Datagram Transport Layer Security (DTLS) 63
Device Firmware Upgrade (DFU) 60
DEVICE-ID 54
DFU-Util
    download link 116
    firmware, flashing 117
    installation link 116
    installing, on Linux 115

installing, on Mac OS 116
installing, on Microsoft Windows 116
reference link 115
direct current (DC) 89

E

electromagnetic (EM) radiation 69
Electron
  about 16, 19
  comparing, with Core 20
  comparing, with Photon 20
  GSM connectivity, reference link 19
  used, for programming model car 102
Extensible Messaging and Presence Protocol
  reference link 63

F

Firebase
  reference link 79, 80
firmware
  about 107
  burning, DFU-Util method 115
  burning, onto device 113
  burning, OTA method used 113
  burning, Particle-CLI used 114
  download link 109
  flashing 108
  history 108
  obtaining 109
  obtaining, by building from source 110
  obtaining, by direct download 109
  reference link 109
flash memory 9
FreeRTOS
  essentials 24, 26
  hardware resources 24, 26
  reference link 23

G

General Purpose Input Output (GPIO) 10
gestures
  used, for moving model car 100
Git binaries, for Mac OS
  reference link 112
Git binaries, for Windows

reference link 112
Google Play Store
  Particle app 29
ground (GND) 94

H

hardware components, for building model car
  65 RPMDC Right Angled motor 90
  about 88
  breadboard 91
  Chassis 91
  jumper wires 91
  L293D 89
  power supply 91
  wheels 88
hardware components, smart kitchen project
  data flow diagrams 70
  hardware motion sensor 68
  RFID reader module RC522-RFID 67
  RFID tags 67
hardware, Particle
  core 16
  electron 16
  photon 16
Homebrew
  reference link 110, 116
HTTP request
  reference link 35
Hyper Text Transfer Protocol (HTTP) 52
Hyper Text Transfer Protocol Secure (HTTPS) 52

I

IC packages
  reference link 106
Integrated Circuit (IC) 9
Integrated Development Environments (IDEs) 8
International Telecommunications Union (ITU)
  reference link 8
Internet Button
  about 23
  reference link 24
Internet of Things (IoT)
  benefits 8
  defining 7
  evolution 8

hardware and software 8
network protocol 11
reference link 7
interrupts
reference link 25
IoT Consortium (IoTC)
reference link 8
IoT development board
about 9, 12
market survey 11
IPSO Alliance
reference link 8
issues, troubleshooting
particle CLI setup and other commands failure
48
web requests failure 48

K

Kevin Ashton
reference link 8
keys, robot() function
connections 97
devices 97
work 97

L

Leap Motion
reference link 87, 100
local server
configuring 59
Particle local server, advantages 58
Particle local server, disadvantages 58
Particle server, installing on local machine 58
setting up 57

M

Machine-to-Machine (M2M) 10
Mailgun
reference link 38
make tool
reference link 111
MFRC522_RFID_Library
reference link 75
microcontroller 9
microprocessor 9

Mobile Backend as a Service (mBaaS) 10
Mode/Setup Button 28
model car, building
hardware components 88
prerequisites 93
model car
code 95
controlling 93
moving, with gestures 100
program, running 99
programming, with Electron 102
module 10
MQ Telemetry Transport (MQTT)
reference link 62, 63

N

Near Field Communication (NFC) 67
Node Package Manager (npm)
about 29
reference link 55
Node.js
reference link 29, 55

O

OASIS
reference link 62
OAuth
reference link 34
OSI model
reference link 11
Other Device node 30
Over-The-Air (OTA) 15

P

P2P architectures
versus client-server 53
P2P network, setting up
Particle board, connecting with VodooSpark 54
Particle board, controlling with keyboard 55
VoodooSpark firmware, flashing 54
P2P network
advantages 53, 54
setting up, for Particle devices 54
Particle CLI
reference link 29

Particle cloud 27
Particle dashboard
  reference link 81
Particle Driver
  installation link 30
Particle mobile application
  reference link 29, 103
Particle online store
  reference link 19
particle setup command 32
Particle Web IDE
  reference link 104
Particle
  benefits 16
  history 15
  reference document link 35
  reference link 14, 16, 85
ParticleJS
  reference link 23
peer-to-peer network architecture 52
peers 52
Photon-Internet Button 27
Photon
  about 16, 18, 27
  communication between 72
  comparing, with Core 20
  comparing, with Electron 20
  connecting 31
  hardware requisites 29
  obtaining 28
  reference link 31
  setting up 28
  software requisites 29
  software setup 29, 30
  technical details 18
PIR
  reference link 68
port 10
prerequisites, for obtaining firmware
  ARM GCC 110
  code, compiling 112
  dependencies, obtaining from source code 112
  Git 112
  Make 111
Procter & Gamble (P&G) 8

PTC
  reference link 14

R
Random Access Memory (RAM) 9
RC522-RFID module
  reference link 67
Read Only Memory (ROM) 9
real-time operating system (RTOS) 10
request 52
Reset Button 28
RFID reader
  reference link 68
RFID
  reference link 8
RGB LED 28
Runtime Environment 29

S
Saleae USB Logic Analyzer
  reference link 85
Seeed Studio
  reference link 68
Serial Peripheral Interface (SPI)
  reference link 68
SigFox 8
smart kitchen project
  hardware components 66
  overview 65
  setup 66
  troubleshooting 84
SMS notification
  sending 83
Software Development Kits (SDKs) 8
Spark Core 17
spark-server
  reference link 58

T
TCP/IP protocol
  reference link 62
traditional client-server architecture 52
troubleshooting
  kitchen project 84
  model car 105

Twilio
  reference link 83
Twitter and e-mail interaction project
  about 34
  button presses, sensing 42
  e-mail, sending 43
  motion, sensing 40
  tweets, sending 43
  Twitter developer account, setting up 34
  web requests, sending with Particle webhooks 35
  webhook, creating 35
  webhooks, listing 36
Twitter and e-mail webhook
  setting up 37
Twitter developer account
  reference link 34
Twitter project
  flow diagram 27

U

UART

  reference link 10

V

VoodooSpark
  reference link 54, 119

W

wake-up pin 19
Web IDE
  about 32
  reference link 32
webhook
  creating 35
  deleting 36
  listing 36
  reference link 35
WebSocket
  reference link 63

Z

Zadig
  reference link 116

57779599R00077

Made in the USA
Lexington, KY
25 November 2016